# Contents

## Series Statement

*Teaching and Learning through the National Curriculum* is a series of books for teachers, student-teachers and others involved in the education of children aged 3 to 15 years. Each book has a main subject focus and is concerned with a single key stage (1, 2 or 3). It provides stimulus and insight for experienced teachers and sound practical advice for those new to the profession. Each is based on three main themes: the key issues, the National Curriculum and information technology.

The first chapter provides an up-to-date analysis of educational matters which often goes beyond the immediate concerns of the National Curriculum. Each author identifies the key issues which warrant systematic attention and which take the reader into some of the important educational issues of the 1990s. The issues vary between subjects and key stages but all reflect what is considered important by the authors who are accomplished practitioners in their respective fields.

The second chapter focuses on National Curriculum matters and each author provides a rationale for a range of teaching strategies appropriate to the subject and key stage. Examples are used to illustrate particular ideas and these are supported by copyright-waived pages for teachers to use in the classroom or for INSET. The main function of this chapter is to provide teachers with examples and illustrations of classroom practice.

The third chapter in each book provides the reader with guidance on information technology for the appropriate subject and key stage. This series aims to bridge the gulf between rhetoric and reality by showing how the teaching and learning of that subject can be enhanced through accessible IT materials.

This series will make an effective contribution to subject-focused teaching and learning at key stages 1, 2 and 3. As a series, it provides an authoritative and up-to-date discussion of the 1995 National Curriculum and sets the issues in a broader framework of teaching and learning.

References and Bibliography are given for further reading.

## Foreword

Fran Martin provides a thorough analysis of geography learning for young children and addresses matters which are of major concern to teachers and others working in this important field. The increasing recognition of the importance of early years learning in circles beyond the teaching profession is a significant feature of the 1990s and I am sure that this book will play its part in supporting enhanced provision across Reception and key stage 1. Another notable recent development is the increased attention being given to subject-focused learning in the early years. This has been stimulated not only by the structure of the National Curriculum but also by a wider recognition that subjects can provide a formal structure for learners of all ages, including those in their early years. Because of its broad scope, geography provides enormous opportunities for teaching and learning in the early years and these are brought out most effectively by Fran Martin in the following pages.

Fran Martin successfully combines a lively description of practical matters which are immediately classroom-focused with a scholarly analysis of theoretical issues which are equally vital for effective classroom practice. The two sides of the same coin are entwined throughout this book and readers will find it useful and stimulating.

**Roger Trend**
*Assistant Director (Initial Professional Studies)*
*School of Education*
*University of Exeter*

Teaching and Learning
through the National Curriculum

Series Editor  Roger Trend

# Teaching Early Years Geography

*Chris Kington Publishing*

CAMBRIDGE

© Fran Martin
ISBN 1 899857 25 7

First published 1995 by
Chris Kington Publishing
27 Rathmore Road
Cambridge CB1 4AB

British Library cataloguing in publication data. A catalogue record for this book is available from the British Library.

Design by Barry Perks Graphic Design
Copy-editing by Carole Drummond, Milestone Editorial

Printed in the United Kingdom by York Publishing Services, 64 Hallfield Road, Layerthorpe, York Y03 7XQ

# Chapter 1: Key Issues

## Key Issue 1: What is Geography and Why Teach It in the Early Years?

### The Nature of Geography

"Geography explores the relationship between the Earth and its peoples through the study of place, space, and environment. Geographers ask the questions where and what; also how and why?" (DES, 1990a). This definition has provided the framework for the geography National Curriculum. Within this definition it is possible to have an image of geography that is aligned with the sciences on the one hand and the humanities on the other. Geography, like science and history, is also concerned with the enquiry process through which certain questions might be asked, data collected, interpreted and evaluated, and possible solutions/answers given. It is important, however, to establish what is unique about geography and to explore how this image of the subject affects the way in which it is taught.

### What is Unique about Geography?

What is it that the study of geography can offer children, in terms of developing their understanding of the world around them, that cannot be gained from the study of other subjects? Geography is the study of people and their environment and the interaction between them. It is concerned with developing a sense of place, the physical and human elements of the place, and how they affect each other and contribute to the character of the place. In its concern for people and places, geography is ideally placed for developing children's values such as international understanding, a concern for the environment, and an awareness of the interdependent nature of the world.

Finally, "geography is concerned with communicating information and ideas through the language of maps" (Sebba, 1995). Maps are the means by which spatial knowledge and understanding are communicated and as such are essential geographical "tools".

### Teaching Geography in the Primary School

Geography is not merely a body of knowledge that has to be imparted to children. It is not just about knowing the names of places, where they are located, what the economy of the area is and so on. Knowledge certainly is important, but equally important is the teacher's role in encouraging children to "be geographers", to ask questions of a geographical nature, to use geographical tools to help find the answers and to attempt to understand the world in the ways a geographer does. "We teach a subject not to produce little living libraries, but to consider matters as a geographer does, to take part in the process of knowledge..." (Bruner, 1966).

### Why Teach Geography in the Early Years?

Since the geography taught now may be significantly different from the geography our pupils' parents learnt at school, it is important to have a rationale for what is taught and how it is taught.

Children are geographers from the moment they begin exploring their environment (Catling, 1978). From a very early age they have a fascination for places, both real and imaginary. They come into contact with people and places on a variety of scales on a daily basis. As a result, all children arrive at school with their own "private geographies" or worlds inside their heads (Bale, 1987). The study of geography can help them to make sense of these private geographies. Few teachers of young children would have difficulty in applying this to places such as the school, a local playground, the nearby shops and people who are known in the local community. However, because of a deep-rooted belief that the most successful early years teaching is done through first-hand experience, some teachers have difficulty in identifying a rationale for the study of distant peoples and places.

This concern will be discussed in greater depth later on (see pages 3 and 5) but it is worth noting at this point that: "encounter need not be direct and local ... it could as well be an encounter with a distant place through a film, or a picture book or a story" (Wiegand, 1993).

At a pragmatic level, geography can develop "life skills" such as those required for planning a journey, choosing an appropriate map and reading it to find the way. The most effective way of showing what geography has to offer, and therefore why it is taught, is to map it out.

| Knowledge | Understanding (Key Concepts) | Skills | Attitudes/Values |
|---|---|---|---|
| Places, their physical and human characteristics. Locality of the school. Contrasting locality. Evidence. | Location. Spatial pattern and distribution. Similarity and difference. Processes and systems. Change and stability. Cause and effect. | Mapwork. Fieldwork. Enquiry, asking and responding to geographical questions. Interpreting a range of sources. Using geographical vocabulary. | Awareness of, and respect for, different lifestyles and cultures. Ability to see others' points of view. Awareness that people's values affect their actions. Concern for quality in the environment. |

*Figure 1.1 Mapping geography.*

## Geographical Content and Processes

Figure 1.1 gives an overview of the knowledge, understanding, skills, attitudes and values that can be developed through geographical study. Each of these is examined in turn.

### Geographical Knowledge

Within the National Curriculum framework there are still several content choices that can be made. These will need to be appropriate for the early years and reflect a balance between that which is known and familiar and that which is more distant and less familiar. Similarly, such choices should reflect a balance between small-scale study that focuses, for example, on a particular building or street and larger-scale studies of a whole locality which give children the opportunity to make generalisations.

The relationship between knowledge and understanding needs to be considered when making content choices. For example, in order to develop an understanding of the spatial distribution of certain human features in the local area, children might learn that homes are generally clustered together (as are shops), whereas post boxes are found singly and dotted about an area. Linked to this is the importance of learning the geographical terminology that is appropriate for this age group. The relationship between language and thought is discussed in Key Issue 4 below.

It is perhaps a truism to state that the knowledge outlined in the National Curriculum of 1995 is not all the geographical content that can be taught in schools. There is considerable freedom to include geographical knowledge that closely reflects the nature of the community within which the school is situated.

### Geographical Understanding

Concepts provide a means of making sense of what is known through organising that knowledge in certain ways. For example, understanding the nature of a place (such as a school) might be done by comparing it with another place (such as a home), by looking at it as a system of inputs and outputs and by considering why it is where it is, the pattern of arrangement of the classrooms, and so on. For further examples of how to develop key geographical concepts, please see Key Issue 4.

### Geographical Skills

The development of geographical skills is a prominent part of the National Curriculum requirements. To be a geographer involves posing certain questions, collecting relevant information from a variety of sources, both first-hand (e.g. through fieldwork) or second-hand (e.g. from maps, photographs, books), interpreting the data collected and presenting findings in an appropriate way (e.g. graphical, through maps, charts and pictures). Further examples are given in Key Issue 4.

### Geographical Attitudes and Values

All children arrive at school with certain attitudes towards people and places. These in part have been developed through the value-system of the home and community, and in part through more indirect contacts with the world (e.g. television). As well as building on positive attitudes, geographical study can also challenge stereotypical views and fulfil its "potentially significant role in creating a better world" (Fien & Gerber, 1988).

In summary, many of the elements that go to make up geography (with the exception, perhaps, of mapwork and spatial understanding) are also present in other subjects (e.g. history and science). It is when you put those individual elements together as a unitary whole that you have the answer to the question "what is geography?". The uniqueness of geography lies in the way that all the elements fit together, it is the study of people and places, their spatial distribution, the interaction between them and the processes involved.

## Key Issue 2: Geography and Young Children's Learning

### How Do Children Learn?

If we have some understanding of how children learn this can be applied to both what we should teach (i.e. the curriculum) and how we should teach it (i.e. teaching approaches and methods). Research into children's development of geographical knowledge, understanding, skills and attitudes has very clear implications for primary practice. The study of distant places has often been considered inappropriate for young children because of their inability to conceive large distances. However, there are two distinct aspects to developing geographical knowledge and understanding of places:

1. Knowing and understanding where and how far away a place is – i.e. locational knowledge and spatial understanding.
2. Knowing and understanding that there are other places in the world which are in some ways the same as, and in some ways different from, the places in which we live.

The former is a complex concept for young children to grasp and is often best developed within a local study framework where locations and distances of known features can be considered. The latter is about developing a sense of place and therefore involves drawing comparisons between one place and another. It is well within the grasp of young children and can be very successfully taught using a variety of approaches.

For this reason, ideas about how children learn in geography will first be considered in a local context and then within the context of distant places.

### Children's Learning in a Local Context

Matthews (1992) cites several pieces of research that give an interesting insight into how young children develop an understanding of their local environment. Briefly, the range (distance) of encounters in the environment increases with age, as one would expect, and the chief factors affecting this range are:

1. Physical ability, e.g. the ability to ride a bike.
2. Parental attitudes, e.g. whether it is safe for a child to play outdoors.
3. The physical nature of the environment, e.g. barriers such as a busy main road, river, etc.

There were also *gender* differences noticed in the *type* and *range* of play. Boys' play is more exploratory and large-scale, while girls' is more home-oriented and small-scale. Also, boys are often given more freedom of range than girls. It is hardly surprising, therefore, to find that boys consistently out-perform girls from an early age in their ability to represent areas in mapped form. For example, Siegal and Schadler (1977) in Matthews (1992) have shown that boys were far more accurate than girls at placing model furniture in the correct position within a scaled reproduction of their classroom.

Research by Matthews (1992) confirms that boys' maps are broader in concept, more detailed and more accurate than girls' maps. There are clear implications for teaching in terms of the extra experiences offered to girls (large-scale play which encourages physical manipulation and exploration of the environment) and in the way children are grouped when working on mapping tasks – should they be of mixed gender or boys/girls only?

Research has also been described (Matthews, 1992; Palmer, 1994) regarding the ways in which we ask children to describe their environment. Typically this involves a verbal description or the drawing of a map, both of which involve free recall. However, it is suggested that: "Young children simply lack the motor skills and semantic abilities to provide clear route descriptions by graphic and verbal recall" (Matthews, 1992). If the children's mapping of routes, etc., is carefully structured through the use of aerial photographs, large-scale plans, 3-D modelling and so on, all of these techniques have been shown to enhance the levels of achievement. Examples of this can be seen in Figures 1.2 and 1.3 below. Figure 1.2 shows maps of the locality drawn by Year 2 children. Map A is drawn by a girl and Map B by a boy. Figure 1.3, shows two further locality maps drawn by the same children, Map C by a girl and Map D by a boy. Although drawn on the same day, the second maps were done after some structured input from the teacher using a set of symbols that could be arranged on a base map. The small group of children discussed the relative positions of the features at length before being asked to draw their second map. This makes an interesting comparison.

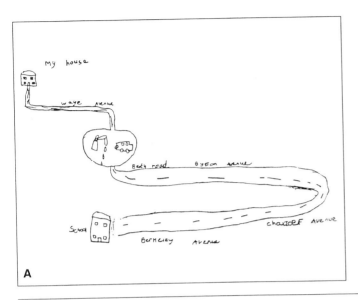

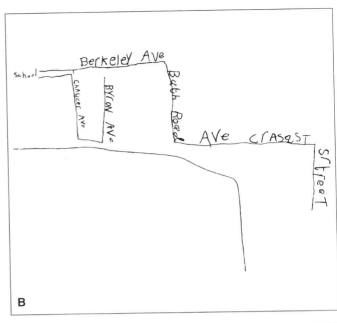

*Figure 1.2 Children's maps before teacher input.*

Research shows that those children who are able to represent their environment in mapped form tend also to have a much greater understanding of location, spatial distribution and pattern. The current section is largely devoted to competence in mapping.

There is further debate about the developmental sequence of spatial understanding (Matthews, 1992; Palmer, 1994; Wiegand, 1993). Whether children move in a linear way from one stage to the next (see Figure 1.4) is now under question. Although children, in general, at the age of 4 to 5 years show many similarities in the way they draw maps, as do many 7 to 8-year-olds, it is unwise to generalise from this that all children move through the "stages" in the same sequence or at the same rate.

### Children's Learning and Distant Places

Children come into contact with people and places beyond their direct experience on a regular basis. This indirect contact includes television, holidays, books, toys, food and

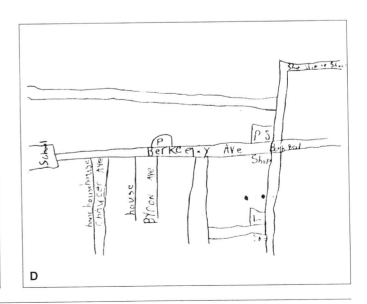

*Figure 1.3 Children's maps after teacher input.*

| | Level 1 | Level 2 | Level 3 |
|---|---|---|---|
| **Location** | Use positional vocab: on, under, in front, behind. Follow directions: up, down, left, right. | Follow directions: north, south, east, west. | Use letter/number coordinates on simple grids. Use 8 points of the compass and relate to directions of features in school. |
| **Symbols** | Draw imaginary maps using own symbols. | Use class-agreed symbols on simple group maps and own maps. | Show need for a key and uniformity in symbols. Use standard symbols. |
| **Scale** | Order objects by size. Use terms like bigger, smaller than. | Draw objects on a table to scale, using squared paper. | Using squared paper, draw simple plan of classroom on scale 1 cm²:1 m². |
| **Perspective** | Use model layouts and playmats. Draw round objects to show plan view. Use plans to make layouts of model farm, etc. | Look down on objects to make plan. Match aerial photos to objects. | Draw sketch map from high viewpoint if possible, or of model village or farm. |
| **Style** | Extract information from picture maps. Use globes. | Identify land/sea on globes. Use teacher-drawn base-maps and large scale OS maps, postcard maps. | Identify features on aerial photos. Have a collection of maps to interpret – tourist maps, OS maps. |
| **Drawing** | Draw picture maps of imaginary places and from stories, e.g. "The Three Little Pigs". Mark route taken by pigs and wolf. | Make representations of real and imaginary places. Draw route to school. | Make map of short route showing features in correct order. Draw plans of bedroom, play area, etc. |
| **Map use** | Talk about own picture map. | Follow route using a plan. Relate plan of school to actual building(s) or photos of buildings. | Use large-scale map outside. Use maps of other localities. |

*Figure 1.4 Developing mapwork skills (adapted from Morgan, 1991).*

so on. Children are therefore gaining knowledge about, and forming attitudes towards, other people, places and cultures from an early age. Research shows that there is a strong and complex link between knowledge and attitude formation (Wiegand, 1992; Palmer, 1994). There is some evidence to suggest that attitudes are learned first: "If the attitude is learned first, this might predispose the child to acquire only that information that confirms the attitudes that are already held" (Wiegand, 1992).

In studying distant places, therefore, teachers should be concerned with challenging certain attitudes, as well as fostering others. It is important, therefore, to consider carefully the images of distant places that we present to children. For example, it has been shown that if the images contrast strongly with the child's own experience (e.g. pictures or photos stressing differences) then negative attitudes can be increased (Wiegand, 1992). Perhaps it is advisable to begin with focusing on similarities – children living in families, going to school, doing chores around the house, playing – and then consider differences in the light of, for example, the impact of weather and landscape. "Learning about places is about promoting understanding, developing a sense of commonality ... recognising similarities and valuing and celebrating diversity" (Catling, 1995).

## Key Issue 3: Planning a Geography Curriculum

### Principles to Guide Curriculum Planning

Traditionally the early years curriculum, including geography, has followed a path from: known to unknown, simple to complex, concrete to abstract, nearby to distant. At the same time it is generally accepted that young children learn most effectively when work is based on their own experiences. In general, children's experiences have been interpreted in terms of what they know. This has led to curriculum planning which focuses on content rather than processes (skills, concepts and attitudes). The difficulty with using children's knowledge as the main guide for planning is that it can be very restricting at one level (the here and the now predominate) and too broad at another level. When deciding what to teach about a locality, for example, the possibilities are endless on what should be included and what excluded. Curriculum areas such as English, maths, music, design and technology, and art focus mainly on the skills and understanding which children need to develop in order to achieve mastery of the subject. The processes are therefore already at the forefront when planning is undertaken. This is the *process approach* to curriculum planning. Geography, with its body of knowledge, is often treated in a different way. Planning frequently identifies knowledge to be covered by use of a topic web which is then divided into chunks to be covered week by week. The problem with planning in this way is that content links can

be tenuous. Brainstorming may lead to content overload unless criteria are identified for selection.

A model which uses process rather than content to guide curriculum planning will help to shift the focus from knowledge to *skills and understanding* when deciding what areas to cover. In this way a teacher might identify that pupils need to develop an ability to use maps to help develop their understanding of similarities and differences between areas. This would seem to make a far more logical starting point for planning a topic than "what content shall we teach next?", the selection of which may be arbitrary. The National Curriculum has attempted to focus more on geographical processes but, up until now, the programme of study was largely content-bound and did not readily lend itself to a process-based approach to planning. The new Order opens up planning opportunities and this is discussed further in Chapter 2.

Another reason for taking a process approach to curriculum planning is that it enables teachers to use a child's skills and understanding as the starting point for building on his or her own experiences. For example, most children will have a rudimentary understanding of location, cause and consequence, similarity and difference, etc., when they come to school. If this is used as one of the criteria for selecting content we are then "freed from the constraint of believing that new knowledge cannot be meaningfully introduced except by some content association with knowledge gained from the child's present experience" (Egan, 1988). Figure 1.5 is a list of criteria that can be used to guide curriculum

| Points to Consider when Planning the Whole Curriculum | Points to Consider that Are More Specific to Geography |
|---|---|
| 1. Are the topics subject-based or cross-curricular? <br><br> 2. Are the units of work termly or half-termly? Many schools choose one or other of these options. With younger children, a topic focus over a shorter period of time is advisable. Some aspects might last for longer than a term, e.g. recording the weather on a daily basis. <br><br> 3. Ensure progression in terms of both content (knowledge) and processes (skills and concepts). <br><br> 4. Ensure continuity of approach (active, enquiring, and variety of teaching methods) both within the key stage and between pre-school and KS2. <br><br> 5. Over the year and the key stage rotate the main focus for each topic or unit of work (i.e. consider the place of all subjects). | 6. Are the geography units blocked or elongated? Some schools prefer to "block" time available for geography so that one term might have a major geographical focus, while in the next term opportunities for geography are negligible and history, say has the main focus. For the early years, it is more appropriate to have a geographical element to every topic so that children have "repeated opportunities to talk and think geography in a manageable way" (Mackintosh, 1995). <br><br> 7. Try to provide a balance each year between place and thematic study, breadth, and depth in terms of knowledge, understanding, skills and attitudes. <br><br> 8. Although most place study will be small-scale, provide some opportunities for studies at broader scales (and this increasingly as children move through the key stage), e.g. putting the place in its broader context. <br><br> 9. Be aware at this stage what opportunities there are for fieldwork, information technology and other cross-curricular dimensions such as multi-ethnic education. |

*Figure 1.5 Points to consider in curriculum planning.*

planning and which has been drawn up in the light of the above comments.

## The Spiral Curriculum

"Bruner's concept of a spiral curriculum suggests that in early childhood children should be introduced to key ideas and concepts in a simple form, and should meet them again in more highly developed forms ... with each encounter leading to a more sophisticated understanding" (Mackintosh, 1995). The National Curriculum for Geography (DFE, 1995a) follows this model in its focus on strands that are revisited at various points through the key stages (see Chapter 2). What is appealing about the model is that, with its focus on "key ideas and concepts", it is another means of providing progression in children's learning. It also supports the thinking behind points 3 and 6 in Figure 1.5. The spiral curriculum shown in Figure 1.6 follows the principle of revisiting topics but studying them in increasing depth at each stage. Within this model it is envisaged that children will alternate activities that are demanding and take them a step further in their thinking with those that serve to consolidate learning and allow children to explore new possibilities within a known situation.

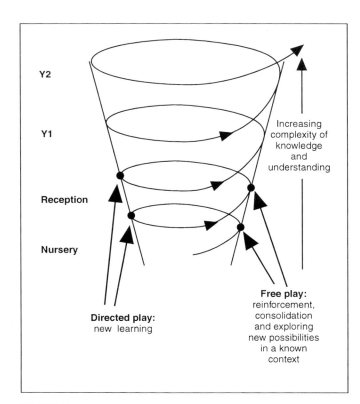

*Figure 1.6 The spiral curriculum.*

## Cross-curricular Links

It is established good practice in the early years for the curriculum to be organised as topics within which links are made between curriculum areas. The National Curriculum has made planning through topics more difficult because of the specific content demands of the various subjects. However, teachers have been at pains to maintain an integrated approach and to build on what they know to be an effective way of planning in key stage 1. The Plowden Report recognised that: "the learning of young children is not naturally differentiated, their view of the world is not divided into neat compartments" (Plowden, 1967). Other reasons for an integrated approach are:

1. Studying a problem, issue or phenomenon through more than one subject can lead to greater depth of understanding. For instance, developing an understanding of the nature of water might involve looking at its properties (science) and linking them to its uses (geography and technology).
2. Geography can provide the context for the development of subjects such as maths, English and art. For example a study of weather might include collecting data and making charts (application of maths), giving weather forecasts or writing weather reports (speaking and listening, writing for a purpose) and drawing where the rain goes when it falls on the playground (recording observations).
3. At a pragmatic level, integrating subjects is an effective use of time. Given the amount of content in the National Curriculum, it is helpful if topics, and specific activities within those topics, can relate to more than one subject at the same time.

However, it is important that, within the integrated framework, subjects keep their distinctiveness at the planning stage. This ensures that those elements that are unique to the subject are identified, and that a balance is achieved across those elements over the key stage. To plan subjects separately (but not in isolation from each other) does not mean that they have to be taught separately at all times. There are times when it is beneficial for children to know when they are studying geography, as opposed to history or science. The awareness is important because key stage 1 provides the foundation for work at key stages 2 and 3. The earlier the uniqueness of each subject is identified and made overt in teaching, the easier it is to provide continuity of experience across all key stages.

There is also some evidence to suggest that making children aware of the nature of a subject and its skills and knowledge can lead to higher levels of achievement. This is known as metacognition or "helping children to be conscious of what they know and can do and then teaching them how to draw purposefully on that knowledge and to deploy it when working on problems" (Knight, 1993). This idea links with the need to establish what "private geographies" children hold when they arrive at school (Bale, 1987). Often these will incorporate misconceptions of the world about them which will need to be identified and acknowledged before purposeful teaching and development of a conceptual framework can take place.

*Using Topic Webs*

Are topic webs still useful as a planning tool? In the past topic webs "had a central starting point, which was brainstormed with unlimited choice, and therefore had unpredictable outcomes" (Foley & Janikoun, 1992). This style of planning does not ensure continuity or progression, does not address processes, and is generally too broad to allow for depth of study. However, topic webs can be useful if the planning style moves away from the brainstorm approach and focuses on making *meaningful* links between subjects and topics. Meaningful links will be those that focus on process as much as content. They will reflect the thinking in points 1–3 of Figure 1.5 and could result in topic webs of the following nature:

1. A single-subject focus at the centre of the topic where other subjects support and enhance understanding in the central subject (Figure 1.7). In this example the geography is planned first and the emphasis is therefore on *where* we play, and therefore fostering an understanding of *location*, rather than what we play with. The links with other subjects have been chosen because they add depth to this type of understanding.
2. A multi-subject focus where all subjects have a roughly equal role in providing breadth and depth of understanding to a central issue or theme (Figure 1.8). In this case links are intended to support the development of the central theme.

Palmer (1994) suggests an additional method whereby a topic can be planned on three webs – one for knowledge/content, one for concepts/attitudes and one for skills – or on one web with the three aspects colour-coded.

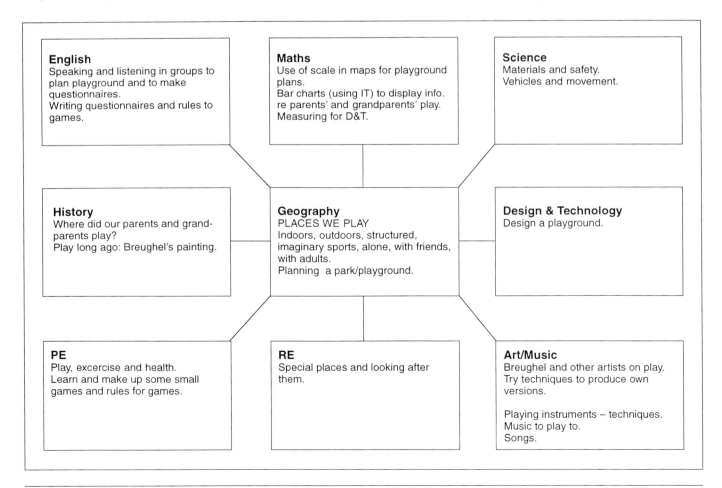

**English**
Speaking and listening in groups to plan playground and to make questionnaires.
Writing questionnaires and rules to games.

**Maths**
Use of scale in maps for playground plans.
Bar charts (using IT) to display info. re parents' and grandparents' play.
Measuring for D&T.

**Science**
Materials and safety.
Vehicles and movement.

**History**
Where did our parents and grandparents play?
Play long ago: Breughel's painting.

**Geography**
PLACES WE PLAY
Indoors, outdoors, structured, imaginary sports, alone, with friends, with adults.
Planning a park/playground.

**Design & Technology**
Design a playground.

**PE**
Play, excercise and health.
Learn and make up some small games and rules for games.

**RE**
Special places and looking after them.

**Art/Music**
Breughel and other artists on play.
Try techniques to produce own versions.

Playing instruments – techniques.
Music to play to.
Songs.

*Figure 1.7 Topic web with a single-subject focus.*

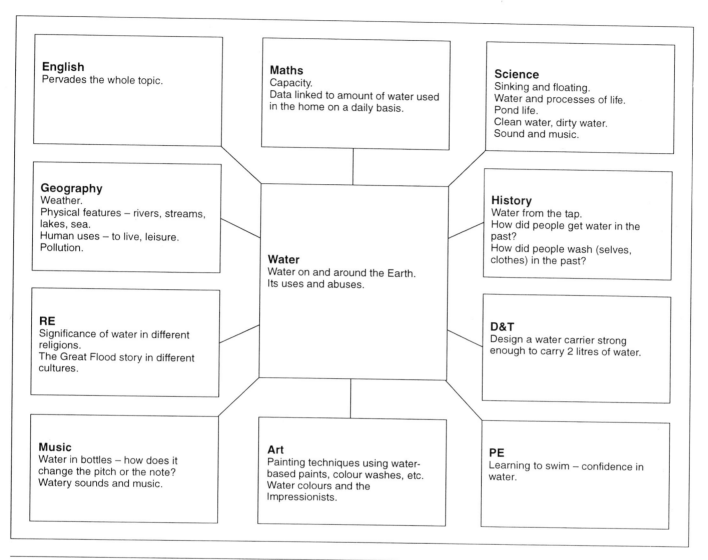

*Figure 1.8 Topic web with a multi-subject focus.*

## Key Issue 4: Teaching Approaches and Methods

### Early Years Geography and Active Learning

Active learning is just what it suggests: an approach to teaching in which the children are actively engaged in the learning process. The rationale behind this is based on research that shows: "What I hear I forget, what I see I remember, what I do I understand" (an ancient Chinese proverb). This has been part of early years practice for many years but it does not mean that children have to be *physically* active in, for example, manipulating concrete objects. There are certainly situations, such as developing early map skills through model-making, where this is appropriate. However, there are also times when being active can mean "manipu-

lating" information and ideas through discussion in order to understand them.

There are many types of learning activity which therefore may or may not involve physical activity. The point is that the activity is fundamentally a *cognitive* process. The advantages of active learning are:

1. Children have more responsibility for their own learning and can participate at their own level.
2. It is flexible and gives children the opportunity to learn through discovery.
3. It can provide a balance between co-operative groupwork and individual work.
4. Communication or presentation of ideas can be done in a variety of ways – such as written, pictorial, verbal, graphical or in the form of a model.

A belief in the power of active learning to stimulate cognitive activity and enhance children's achievements provides the basis for the following examples of geographical teaching approaches: the enquiry process; using maps in the early years; asking geographical questions; doing fieldwork at key stage 1; using play and role-play; using pictures and photographs; and using stories in geography. Although the approaches are listed separately, it will be seen that some activities make use of more than one approach. For example, enquiry might be used in the classroom using photographs or in the locality as part of fieldwork.

## The Enquiry Process

Teaching geography in the early years, encouraging children to be 'geographers', is all about being active. One of the key ways in which this is achieved is through the enquiry process. "An enquiry approach ... may be defined as one in which the teacher assists pupils to develop the abilities to ask questions and to seek to answer them through investigative work" (DES, 1990a).

Figure 1.9, showing the enquiry process, has been adapted from the NCC INSET Resources (NCC, 1993). Figure 1.10 shows how this might be applied to a particular investigation with Reception/Year 1 children. Enquiry can form the basis of a particular lesson or activity, or it can provide the framework for the geographical element of a whole topic. Supplementary Material 4 is a planning matrix for this approach.

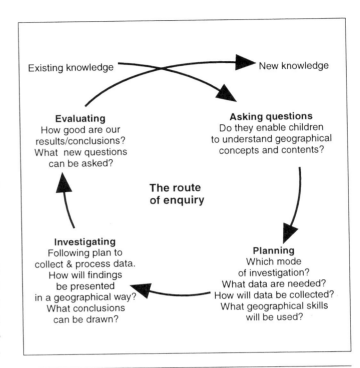

*Figure 1.9 The enquiry process.*

## Using Maps in the Early Years

As mentioned in Key Issue 2, young children are already able to draw their own rudimentary maps and to make interpretations of pre-drawn maps before they start school. It is essential to build on this ability for the following reasons:

| Enquiry Route | Activities | Organisation & Assessment Opportunities |
|---|---|---|
| **Asking questions:** Does our playground have litter? Where does the litter collect? What type of litter is it? | Walk round the playground. Discussion. | Teacher and whole class. |
| **Planning:** How can we find out what litter there is and where it is? How will we record the information? | Discussion. Design sheet for recording where litter is (map & symbols). Collecting and bagging examples of litter. | Whole class. Small groups with adult direction. |
| **Investigating:** Was the litter all in the same place? Where was it most? What was the main type of litter found? | Display map, bar charts, litter in sets, etc. Discuss findings. | Small groups, teacher-led. Small groups and whole class. |
| **Evaluating:** Why does litter collect in certain places? What can be done about it? | Discuss and refer back to key questions. Design posters to encourage people to use bins. | Whole class. Individual work. |

*Figure 1.10 Using enquiry for an investigation into litter.*

1. Maps are a key source of geographical information.
2. Using maps and plans on a regular basis helps children to understand that they are a two-dimensional representation of a three-dimensional world.
3. Maps, altases and globes hold a natural fascination for many young children. Atlases kept in the book corner will often be pored over during times of silent reading or free choice.
4. Using real, large-scale maps and plans of known places can enhance children's abilities to notice spatial patterns and to draw more accurate maps themselves.
5. Maps are usually the most appropriate way for children to communicate spatial knowledge and understanding.

Supplementary Materials 10 and 11 give examples of some specific mapping activities.

## Asking Geographical Questions

Young children learn through *action* and *talk*. Discussion with young children is one of the prime ways in which they develop understanding and much of this discussion will be prompted by questions posed either by the teacher or by the child. In order to express geographical ideas children will also need to learn and use geographical vocabulary. Figure 1.11 gives examples of the vocabulary appropriate at key stage 1. Teacher-led questioning can initiate a line of enquiry or encourage children to reflect on findings and draw conclusions. At their best, these questions are a mixture of open and closed ones, depending on the purpose or aim; they encourage children to reason, make judgements, reflect, interpret and ask more questions; and they encourage children to reorganise knowledge by making comparisons, predicting, evaluating, analysing and applying what is known to new situations.

It is often necessary for a two-tier level of questioning to be used. Again, this can be applied to the use of key questions to guide a topic or it can be a pattern followed as part of a particular activity, e.g. when drawing conclusions. Questions at the *first* level are to do with knowledge and are concerned with naming, description and memory recall:

1. Where is this place?
2. What is this place like?

Questions at the *second* level demand reorganisation of what is known, noticing patterns, giving explanations and making predictions:

1. Why is this place as it is?
2. What physical and/or human processes caused it to be like this?
3. How is it connected to other places?
4. How is it changing?
5. How might it change?
6. What is it like to be in this place?
7. How is this place similar to, or different from, another place?

| Place | Location | Map, plan, globe, area, position, near, far, left, right, up, down, north, south, east, west |
|---|---|---|
| **Physical geography** | Landscape | Hill, slope, steep, gentle, valley, mountain, wood, forest, land, rock, soil. |
| | Rivers | River, stream, lake, sea, waves, pond, beach. |
| | Weather | Weather, wind, rain, cloud, frost, ice, storm, snow, sunshine, season, summer, autumn, winter, spring. |
| **Human geography** | Houses | Cottage, terraced, semi-detached, flat, bungalow, mobile home, houseboat, estate. |
| | Settlements | Village, town, city, settlement. |
| | Transport | Path, alley, road, motorway, railway, canal, airport, bridge, tunnel, pedestrian, motorist, journey. |
| | Shops | Corner shop, shopping centre, supermarket, trading estate. |
| | Services | Post office, library, hospital, doctor's surgery, fire station, police station. |
| | Work places | Farm, factory, office, shop, school, garage. |
| | Leisure facilities | Park, museum, cinema, sports centre, swimming pool. |
| **Environmental geography** | Quality | Attractive, unattractive, tidy, litter, noisy, quiet. |
| | Issues | Pedestrianisation, cycle lanes, play areas, waste areas. |

*Figure 1.11 Examples of geographical vocabulary for key stage 1 (adapted from NCC, 1993, and Schoffham, 1995).*

Often the full learning potential of a highly stimulating activity is lost because time is not given at the end for teacher-led questions that help children to reflect and draw conclusions. Content may be learnt, skills may be developed, but understanding does not always follow. Children may not have developed their conceptual framework to accommodate future learning. Figure 1.12 shows an example of a possible line of questioning which draws on a Year 2 study of a local cluster of shops. Fieldwork has established: what type of shops there are; that some are closed and have been empty for some time; that people now need to travel further for these goods. Children also need to develop gradually the ability to ask their own geographical questions. This is because:

1. Questioning helps children to become independent learners.
2. Developing their own lines of enquiry gives children a sense of involvement in the work and is therefore motivating.
3. Children's own questions can often stimulate a line of enquiry the teacher might not have thought of.
4. Children's questions are a good indicator of their present level of knowledge and understanding (see Chapter 2, Section 4, for further detail).
5. Asking questions is part of the enquiry process and therefore a requirement of the National Curriculum.

It is therefore important to give time on a regular basis for children's questions and to show that they are valued by following them up and incorporating them in the study, where appropriate. Some ways of encouraging children to ask questions are:

1. At the beginning of a topic, ask children what they would like to know about the subject.
2. Develop questionnaires together in groups or as a whole class.
3. Ask questions about photographs (see text on using pictures and photographs below).
4. Ask questions about each other, e.g. when a child is talking about a place he or she visited recently.
5. In groups, ask questions about a geographical artefact (a child or an adult can act as scribe).

## Doing Fieldwork at Key Stage 1

Fieldwork is one of the key ways in which children conduct geographical study, particularly at key stage 1 with its emphasis on exploration of the immediate environment. It enables children to learn about their world through direct experience and practical activities. The most important thing to remember about fieldwork is that it should give children the opportunity to gather information and to explore, observe and discover things that cannot be achieved in the classroom. In this way it can support geographical study in several ways:

---

**Questions to Establish Knowledge**

1. How many shops are there?
2. How many have closed down?
3. Which shops have closed down?
4. What did they sell?
5. Are there other shops in the street that sell the same things?

| Questions to Develop Understanding | Concept Developed |
|---|---|
| 1. Why do you think these shops have closed? | Cause |
| 2. Do people mind? | Effect |
| 3. Where do they go to buy these goods instead? | Effect and location |
| 4. Do most people go to the same place? | Location, spatial pattern |
| 5. How do they get there? | Connections between places |
| 6. Is it difficult for some people to get there? | Location, effect |
| 7. Who do you think decided that the shops should close? | Process of decision-making |
| 8. Why do you think she/he/they made that decision? | Causes |
| 9. How do you feel the shoppers feel about the shops closing down? | Effects |
| 10. How do you feel the shopkeepers feel about the shops closing down? | Effects |
| 11. What other things would you like to find out now? | Enquiry |

*Figure 1.12 Teacher-led questions on local shops after fieldwork.*

1. It can be a major focus as part of a local study in which case several field visits may be necessary. (A single visit may be sufficient to support learning in a theme such as transport.)
2. It can be done on a daily basis to collect data, for example, on a topic on weather.
3. It can be small scale – focusing on a particular building, or part of a river or street.
4. It can be large scale – different groups can focus on different areas and gradually build up a picture of the whole area.
5. It makes use of the enquiry process – information collected can be processed and developed back in school.
6. It gives children the opportunity to apply and develop geographical skills, e.g. using maps to follow a route, locate places or record information.

To make most effective use of fieldwork it is essential that the planning undertaken beforehand is detailed and rigorous. Figure 1.13 indicates steps to follow when planning fieldwork. Further detailed information on planning and conducting fieldwork can be found in May et al. (1993) and May & Cook (1993).

## Using Play and Role-Play

Structured or purposeful play is widely recognised as being an important element of early years education (DES, 1989; DES, 1990b; Ball, 1994). This type of play (as opposed to free play which is also important and has its place in the early years classroom) involves the careful selection of materials and equipment as well as adult intervention when appropriate. As well as providing active learning opportunities, children are also able to talk about what they are doing and use vocabulary in a meaningful context. The value of play is summed up in the Rumbold Report (DES, 1990b): "Play is a powerful motivator, encouraging children to be creative and to develop their ideas, understanding and language. Through play, children explore, apply and test out what they know and can do."

Play, therefore, is an ideal context within which geographical skills and understanding can be developed. Here are a few ideas:

1. Modelling the environment using Lego, model building sets, farm sets and so on, helps develop the skill of viewing things from a "bird's-eye" perspective. This can be done through free play, or it can be given structure by asking children to draw round, for example, their farm buildings to produce a map. Making plans of buildings for children to use when setting out models can also help develop position and orientation skills.
2. Play mats for use with model cars, farm animals, etc., are also good for developing early map skills.
3. Role-play is an important way of encouraging children to consider the world from a different viewpoint. This builds the foundation for later work when people's views are considered as motives for their actions and the effect that this might have on the environment.

---

**Pre-visit Planning**

1. At which point during the topic will the fieldwork be appropriate?
2. What do the children need to do/know beforehand?

**Planning the Visit**

3. What is the purpose of the fieldwork? (It is helpful to formulate a key question relating to the focus of the visit, with some supplementary questions that will help to sharpen this focus and define the scope of the enquiry.)
4. What will the learning outcomes be?
5. How will the data be collected? e.g. by survey sheets, pictures, photographs, etc.
6. Will the whole class go together or one group at a time?
7. What adult support, materials and equipment will be needed?

**After the Visit**

8. What will be done with the data collected? Will maps, charts, pictograms or displays be made?
9. What line of questioning will help the children to interpret the data?
10. Will another visit be necessary?

*Figure 1.13 Ten steps for planning fieldwork.*

Children at the beginning of key stage 1 might take on roles during play in the home corner which can be turned into places such as a doctor's surgery, a school office, a shop or a café, depending on the topic at the time, or the children's own choice. Year 2 and Year 3 children can begin to take on roles in a more structured way, expressing views relating to an issue such as "Litter in the Environment". An example of how a role-play on "Planning a park or playground" can be organised is in Supplementary Material 13 and 14.

## Using Pictures and Photographs

"Pupils should be taught to use secondary sources, e.g. pictures, photographs (including aerial photographs)" (DFE, 1995a). As well as providing a means of bringing more distant places into the classroom, pictures and photographs are particularly appropriate for young children because access to stimulus information is not dependent on literacy level. The use of photographs has been well documented (Wiegand, 1992 & 1993; Morgan, 1992; Schoffham & Jewson, 1994). The following sections on photographs and pictures provide some ideas of the types of pictures and photographs that are useful and how they might be used.

### Photographs

A collection of *postcards* can be gradually built up and used for sorting into rural/urban places, seaside/inland places, physical features/human features, and so on. A collection of postcards of a particular place can be displayed to show "the nature and variety of life and environment" (Catling, 1992).

*Photopacks* of more distant places in and beyond the UK (see resources in Section 5 of Chapter 2) are designed to meet the small-scale locality requirements of the National Curriculum. Some focus on particular families as well as aspects of everyday life and features of a distinctive nature. These also attempt to present positive images in a non-stereotypical way.

Children in groups may be asked to choose a photograph and ask questions about the people, features, etc., shown. They can swap the photograph and questions with another group. Which questions can the children answer simply by using the information in the photograph and where can they find the answers to the other questions?

Children can be guided to select a photograph which shows a typical aspect of life, such as a market scene, and compare it with a photograph of a market scene from their own area.

Photographs are an excellent means by which children can record features observed during fieldwork. Photographs taken at different times of the day can reveal patterns such as traffic flow and the number of people in a shopping area.

*Aerial photographs* are useful for beginning mapwork with young children. A selection of vertical and oblique aerial photographs, at different scales, can be provided for the children to browse through. Other activities might include:

1. A child can be asked to name five things that can be seen in a photograph. Then a friend can be asked to do the same. Did they recognise the same things? How did they recognise them?
2. A small group of children can be given a list of things to look for in a photograph.
3. Large-scale aerial photos can be traced over to make a rudimentary map that is then colour coded with a key. (Although the aerial photographs will usually be in colour, there may be times when black and white ones are more appropriate.)

*Satellite images* are becoming available as a resource for geography in primary schools. Although these are more appropriate for key stage 2, some are still useful for familiarisation purposes with key stage 1 (see resources in Section 5 of Chapter 2).

Satellite images of the UK or of Europe can be displayed as A2 size posters and the children can be asked questions such as:

1. Where is the sea?
2. Where is the land?
3. Can you see where mountains are?

### Pictures

Much of what has been said above will apply to the use of pictures. Be aware that pictures, for example picture postcards, will often have been drawn to present a particular view of a place and therefore might not represent a true image. If children are asked to draw their own picture of a place at the beginning of a distant place study, for example, this can give the teacher a very good idea of what images they already have of that place.

Pictures in books, particularly story books, are a very useful source and often present positive images. Unfortunately, artists' impressions in non-fiction books do not always meet the same high standards and so need to be used with caution.

## Using Stories in Geography

Stories have long been accepted as an appropriate resource when teaching young children. Their potential for introducing and developing geographical knowledge and ideas is explored by Palmer (1994) and Norris-Nicholson (1994). Many stories have a strong sense of place and give descriptions using geographical vocabulary. In addition, stories can develop successfully certain types of understanding. Some examples of how this might be done are as follows:

1. Use a story that has a good *description of a place*, including relevant locational vocabulary, as the stimulus for model-making and/or mapwork (see the list of stories in Section 5 of Chapter 2).

2. The "Katie Morag" stories by Mairi Hedderwick (see Section 5 of Chapter 2) are an excellent stimulus for study of a *contrasting locality* within the UK. The Island of Coll (the place in which the stories are set) is depicted in geographical language and in excellent pen and water-colour pictures. This island has also been the subject of a BBC programme for schools, *Words and Pictures* (Spring 1995). There are plenty of opportunities for contrasting lifestyles, physical and human features. The fact that there are also many similarities makes it easy for young children to identify with the characters and, therefore, the context of the story. (For a fuller example see Section 4 of Chapter 2.)

3. For older children there are many stories available that depict *life in areas beyond the UK*. One example of this is *My Grandpa and the Sea* (see the list of stories in Section 5 of Chapter 2) which gives an account of life on St. Lucia in the Caribbean. Children can identify with the central storyline which explores the relationship between a young girl and her grandfather. There is also a strong element of change in their lives linked to technological advances, and the environmental impact of these is explored. The story provides an excellent stimulus for role-play where the views of the grandfather, grandchild and nephew (who represents change) can be explored.

To sum up, there are many different teaching styles and approaches that are appropriate for developing geographical knowledge, skills and understanding. When deciding which style or approach to use within the classroom, teachers will need to think about what the lesson is trying to develop and why, so that the principle of "fitness for purpose" (David et al., 1992) can be achieved. Further detailed discussion of this principle can be found in Section 4 of Chapter 2.

## Key Issue 5: Geography and Pre-School Education

"Good pre-school education leads to immediate and lasting social and educational benefits for all children ... Investment in high-quality and effective early education provides a worthwhile social and economic return to society" (Ball, 1994). Research in the UK and America has repeatedly identified the importance of pre-school education. The significant factors are that this education should be *effective* and of *high quality*. What is it that makes pre-school education effective and of high quality? There are a number of reports on early years education that have emerged in recent years (DES, 1990b; David et al., 1992; Ball, 1994). These show general agreement about the underlying principles that lead to high-quality early years programmes. These principles are:

1. What children *can* do, not what they cannot, should be the starting point for learning.
2. Concrete experience is crucial in helping children move towards abstract thinking.
3. Children should be given the opportunities to explore in situations which have meaning for them.
4. Interaction with the environment includes adults, other children, materials and knowledge. These relationships with peers and adults are of central importance to children's development and indicate the need for a secure learning environment.
5. Learning takes place chiefly through play and talk, in both structured and unstructured situations.
6. Young children learn most effectively when actively involved and interested, and when they are confident in themselves and their ability.
7. A holistic view of the child in which learning, care and emotional support cannot be separated means that the curriculum should not be subject-based; it should be flexible and suited to individual needs.

Since early learning is the "formal and informal learning of young people aged 0–7" (Ball, 1994), these principles could be seen to apply to children's learning throughout key stage 1 and as such they are not at odds with ideas discussed in the key issues above, particularly Key Issue 4. If this is the case, and there is liaison between parents, schools and pre-school teachers, then continuity of experience in the early years can be achieved. However, pre-school provision varies enormously across the UK. Some children will have been to nursery school and perhaps have had a fairly formal education based on the nine areas of learning and experience (DES 1985; DES 1990b). Others will have been to playgroup where the experience might have been less formal. Some children may not have had any pre-school education at all. The implications of this for Reception teachers relate to assessment which is discussed in detail in Section 3 of Chapter 2.

This section will look at the teaching of geography at the pre-school stage. In particular it will examine how geographical knowledge, understanding, skills and attitudes can be developed in a way which is appropriate for pre-school children. The section will finish by discussing the issue of continuity between pre-school education and key stage 1.

An audit of much pre-school work would probably reveal that elements of geography are being covered for much of the time. Children are encouraged to develop their understanding of the world about them – their families and community, their homes and local areas, the people who live there and the type of work they do. This often provides the context for the development of literacy and numeracy skills. Geography, therefore, is not a new subject to pre-school teachers. However, because pre-school teaching is usually based on the holistic view of child development, geography might not be identified as such. It will more often be incorporated into cross-curricular topics which might be organised under the HMI (Her Majesty's Inspectorate) nine areas of learning and experience.

The types of activities that are appropriate for this age-group are the same as those outlined in Key Issue 4, and in Section 4 of Chapter 2. The emphasis in pre-school education is more likely to be on combining action and talk through play opportunities, but essentially the principles which guide teaching approaches will be the same as for key stage 1. Some ideas for activities are now listed under two headings: geographical skills and geographical knowledge and understanding.

## Geographical Skills

These include using maps and plan views, using geographic vocabulary, following directions and making maps.

### Using Maps and Plan Views

Provide a plan of a place setting for children to use in the home corner in order to set things in the correct position. Do the same for table top plans using Logiblock or solid shapes in plan view. Set up a simple arrangement on a table top and ask the children to draw the correct positions on a sheet of paper. Make a collection of photographs which show familiar objects from different viewpoints (overhead, side, oblique) and ask the children to sort them into sets and/or

match to the object. Scott (1994) describes an example of a mapping task.

### Using Geographical Vocabulary

Choose an object in the room and ask the children to try to find out what it is by asking – is it *near* the door, *on* the table or *beside* the sink? Once they are used to this game, children can take it in turn to choose an object. Encourage the children to describe accurately where an object is in the room, rather than pointing.

### Following Directions

Give directions for the children to follow; increase the number in the sequence as they improve. Ask the children to give each other directions (for example, by playing robots – go forward three steps, turn left). PE provides an excellent setting for following directions and using associated vocabulary – go under the bench, climb through the hoop, jump over the box, walk along the bench and climb up and down the wall bars.

### Making Maps

Use a story as a stimulus, for example, *Fantastic Mr Fox* (see the list of stories in Section 5 of Chapter 2). This has the description: "In a valley, on a hill, there was a wood. In the wood there was a tall tree. Under the tree lived...". Using junk modelling materials, the children can make a model of the foxes' home and make a map of the model. A similar activity can be done using Lego, building bricks, Playmobil models and so on. The children can choose what sort of area they wish to model or they can make a model from a pre-drawn map.

## Geographical Knowledge and Understanding

Playmats, model farms, Lego and so on can all be used to make representations of places imagined or real – farm, village, shopping area or street – to increase geographical knowledge and understanding. This can become more structured if done following a visit in which the children were asked to observe certain features carefully.

The home corner can be converted on a fairly regular basis so that the play reflects an aspect of the topic being studied, for example, a tourist office for a topic on journeys or holidays. Set it up with the children as it is important that they help to plan the area in order to establish the change of use more firmly. It also provides motivation to use it in the way you want. As well as brochures, posters, pads, maps, a globe and a computer, children could make a set of cards to represent tickets, with a symbol on each to show the mode of transport. The children would then need to think about the type of ticket they need, according to their destination. Other popular choices for home corner play are: library, doctor's surgery, vet's surgery, hairdresser/barber, school office, shop, café, pizza parlour – the list is endless!

Sand and water areas can be used for modelling physical environments such as hilly areas, coasts and harbours. Water can be poured on to a sand hill to see where rain goes when it falls on the ground. This type of play can become more structured if it follows a group discussion about a particular environment using a large photograph (or picture from a big discussion book) for stimulus.

To conclude, providing continuity of experience from pre-school to key stage 1 is a key issue for some Reception teachers, particularly since the introduction of the National Curriculum. The pressure on Reception teachers to "teach to the National Curriculum" has been great. However, new guidance from SCAA has clearly stated that the programmes of study for key stage 1 have been revised in such a way that they can be taught and assessed in six terms. In other words, there is now no obligation to teach the National Curriculum before Year 1.

The Schools Curriculum Assessment Authority (SCAA) gives the following recommendation: "Reception should have an appropriate curriculum for the pupils in that particular class or school and may or may not include elements from the key stage 1 programme of study" (Makins,1995). Pre-key stage 1 work can therefore reflect all the above aims of high quality pre-school education. OFSTED guidelines for inspectors who judge the quality of pre-key stage 1 work stress the importance of activity, imaginative play, talk, first-hand investigations and use of stories and songs (Makins, 1995).

# Chapter 2: Interpreting and Implementing the National Curriculum

## Section 1: Geography at Key Stage 1

This chapter applies the principles discussed in Chapter 1 to planning early years geography at all levels within the framework of the National Curriculum. The aim is to provide practical guidance, with examples, which links with INSET materials in the Supplementary Materials section. However, before looking at the new Geography Order it is worth examining what advances have been made in geography teaching over the last few years.

Since 1991, when the National Curriculum for geography was first introduced, there has been a significant shift in the emphasis given to geography in the early years and the quality of the teaching and learning. The most recent OFSTED report on geography (1995) singles out key stage 1 as showing elements of particularly good practice. These include:

1. Pupils developing a more sophisticated technical vocabulary.
2. Teaching which challenges pupils with interesting content, activities and a variety of resources.
3. The use of a variety of teaching strategies, e.g. a mix of individual, group and whole class approaches.
4. Good work arising from pupils being stimulated by their personal, practical experiences e.g. using classrooms, school buildings and grounds and the local area to good effect.
5. Schools making a considerable investment in atlases, maps, photographs and reference books and using them well.
6. IT beginning to have a stimulating impact through the use of geographical software.
7. Schools having a geography curriculum that is well constructed (and documented) within a curriculum for the whole school.

As well as building on these aspects of good practice, the OFSTED report (1995) also mentioned elements that could be improved. These were:

1. Pupils had been given insufficient opportunities to draw conclusions and present ideas.
2. There was an over-reliance on commercial worksheets which have their limitations.
3. There was little variation in the tasks set according to ability.
4. Teaching concentrated on one attainment target at a time, rather than integrating them in a study.
5. There was a lack of sufficiently clear schemes of work which clearly identified learning outcomes.
6. Assessment has so far had little influence on the planning of other work.

It is hardly surprising, given the unwieldy nature of the original Order (DES, 1991), that the biggest challenge to teachers has been that of planning a curriculum, within and across key stages, that is coherent and ensures both continuity and progression. Geography, with the amount and detail of prescribed content, has proved particularly difficult to plan, not only on its own, but also within a topic framework that incorporated all the other curriculum areas.

This chapter now examines the changes to the Geography Order and the effect they will have on planning at a variety of levels, from whole school to individual activities. All suggestions for building on and improving current practice will be made in the light of the key issues discussed in Chapter 1, and the comments above from the OFSTED report.

### The National Curriculum for Geography

Essentially the nature of geography in the primary school, as defined in the National Curriculum (DES, 1991) remains unchanged. It consists of skills, places and themes which can be represented in a cube form (see Figure 2.1). The geographical element of a topic will, in effect, take a slice of the cube so that skills, place and thematic study may be integrated and not taught in isolation of each other. It may be possible for a topic to have the major focus on a place (line a – b on Figure 2.1) or on an environmental theme (line c – d on Figure 2.1) but in either case the geographical skills of enquiry, mapping and fieldwork will form an integral part of the topic (see Supplementary Material 2). However

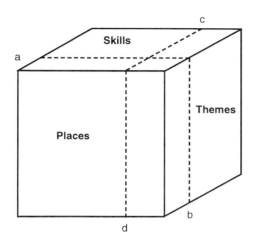

*Figure 2.1 The cube model.*

there are significant changes to the geography curriculum and these are now examined.

## Significant Changes 1991 – 1995

Figure 2.2 outlines the requirement for key stage 1 geography (DFE, 1995a). The differences between this and the 1991 version (DES) are examined under the following

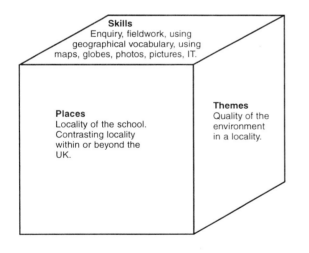

*Figure 2.2 Geography at key stage 1 (1995).*

headings: layout of the document, programmes of study, attainment targets and level descriptions, time allocations, and special educational needs.

## Layout of the Document

Apart from the obvious difference in size (at last it is possible to fit all documents into one school bag!) there are three other significant changes to the layout of the document:

1. The programmes of study are the first thing you come across (instead of the attainment targets, as previously) placing them firmly at the forefront of planning.
2. There is only one attainment target, geography, which appears at the end of the document.
3. The statements of attainment are replaced by level descriptions.

## Key Stage 1 Programme of Study

The content has been severely reduced at key stage 1. This reduction has been achieved partly by excluding overlap with other subjects (e.g. rocks and soils in science) but also by reducing the number of localities from three to two, and the themes from three to one (see Figure 2.3).

| 1991 Order:<br>Range of skills | 1995 Order:<br>Range of skills |
| --- | --- |
| Places:<br>Locality of school.<br>Contrasting UK locality.<br>Locality beyond UK.<br>(Locational knowledge –<br>Maps A & C). | Places:<br>Locality of school.<br>Contrasting locality within or<br>beyond UK.<br>(Locational knowledge –<br>countries of the UK). |
| Themes:<br>Physical.<br>Human.<br>Environmental. | Themes:<br>Quality of the environment in a<br>locality. |

*Figure 2.3 Changes in key stage 1 geography 1991–1995.*

"Freedom to avoid an overseas locality study is a sad loss for young children" (Morgan, 1995). Given the discussion in Chapter 1, particularly in Key Issue 2, there is strong justification for retaining locality study at three different levels. Children need the opportunity to study another part of the UK in order to help them put their own area into some sort of context. Whatever area they live in, children also come into contact with the world beyond the UK and it is important for them to incorporate this into their studies in order to develop knowledge and attitudes as well as counteract stereotypes. The section on planning takes this into account.

The reduction to a single environmental theme does not mean that the physical and human themes have disappeared from key stage 1. There is now no longer a *requirement* for physical and human themes to form the major focus for a study, but knowledge and understanding of physical and human features and processes will continue to be taught through place study.

*Attainment Target and Level Descriptions*

Level descriptions, replacing the former statements of attainment, are paragraphs which teachers use to match against the children's performance at *the end of each key stage*. The intention is that this should be a "best fit" match which allows teachers to exercise their own professional judgement.

*Time Allocations*

The amount of time that schools must devote to geographical study is a minimum of 5 per cent, or 36 hours per year. Minimum is stressed because there is now up to one day a week available for teachers to use at their own discretion. How teachers or schools decide to use this time is entirely up to them but one way at key stage 1 might be to ensure that locality study beyond the UK is retained, along with the aims of values education.

*Special Educational Needs*

"For the small number of pupils who may need the provision, material may be selected from earlier or later key stages" (DFE, 1995a). This statement appears at the beginning of the new Geography Order. The provision is to "enable individual pupils to progress and demonstrate achievement". Otherwise the programmes of study for key stage 1 and key stage 2 have been designed in such a way that there is "content suitable for pupils working towards level 1" (Morgan, 1995).

At key stage 1, provision for children with special needs is likely to follow a similar path to that for all children, with the emphasis being very much on using children's first-hand experiences as the basis for developing geographical skills and understanding. The means by which this will be done is chiefly through talk.

"... the more serious the learning difficulties the more structured must be the approach and smaller the steps" (Smith & Richardson, 1995). Similar content, skills and understanding will therefore be taught, but in smaller chunks and at a slower pace. Input will need to be carefully structured to allow the vocabulary to develop so that children can demonstrate geographical learning. Smith and Richardson (1995) suggest that this will mean drawing up "word lists relevant to the current topic", something that is already a part of good practice in the early years.

In addition, schools will have to make provision for pupils with disabilities of hearing, sight and mobility. This provision will include allowing equal access to practical activities within and beyond the school. Figure 2.4 outlines a set of principles for increasing access to geography:

---

**Increasing Access to Geography**

1. Seek relevance, for example, through developing activities which take account of pupil's interests and experiences.

2. Take every opportunity to use geographical language across the curriculum, for example, up, down, behind, near and far.

3. Look for opportunities to address individual pupil's priorities within geographical activities, for example, communication skills or mobility within fieldwork activities.

4. Use a variety of resources, for example, video, objects, photographs, maps, other people, buildings and sites.

5. Vary the teaching approaches as much as possible, using drama, information technology, and working individually, in pairs, small groups or as a whole class.

6. Share the purposes of sessions with pupils.

7. Invite pupils to record information, responses and reflections, using drawing, models, photographs, symbols, computers or tape recorders, as appropriate.

8. Use total communication such as symbols, signing and Braille to increase pupils' access to activities.

---

*Figure 2.4 Principles for increasing access to geography (Sebba, 1995).*

## The Implications of Key Stage 1 Changes

With the lack of detail that is needed to "flesh out" the context of the new Geography Order, there is a danger that the old Order will continue to be used because teachers are at least used to it! The earlier document certainly will be a useful source of reference for some teachers, but good practice involves the use of a wide range of source material. The biggest challenge now is going to be interpreting the intentions of the new Order and using it for *Planning* and *Assessment*. The implications are now considered.

## Section 2: The Geography Order and Planning at Key Stage 1

A range of terms is commonly used to refer to different aspects of planning or to planning at different scales: a key stage plan, a curriculum plan, a unit of work, and a scheme of work. It is important to define these terms before strategies for planning within them can be considered. Basically, each refers to a different level of planning, each of which will involve a different combination of the school's staff from all staff down to individuals or year teams. Figure 2.5 shows how these levels work. It is up to each school exactly how these planning levels will be tackled and the matrix merely gives suggestions. SCAA guidelines will also need to be consulted, such as *Planning the Curriculum at Key Stages 1 and 2* (SCAA, 1995). It is notable how frequently geography appears in the Making Links section – four out of six examples, *more than any other subject*.

| Planning level | What is involved? | Who is involved? | How often? |
|---|---|---|---|
| 1. Key stage plan | Devising a series of topics for KS1 that incorporates all areas of the curriculum, but particularly the subject knowledge for science, geography and history. This plan should ensure continuity and progression, by referring to PoS and LDs.<br>Topics may have a single-subject focus or a multi-subject focus. | All staff. | Once, then reviewed as necessary. |
| 2. Topic web | Meaningful links between subjects will be explored, including opportunities for IT and multi-ethnic education. | Year groups and subject co-ordinators. | Yearly. |
| 3. Topic curriculum plan | For each topic a curriculum plan will be devised that shows what will be covered in each subject during each week over the period of 6–10 weeks (depending on whether topics are half-termly or termly). | Year groups and subject co-ordinators. | Termly. |
| 4. Subject curriculum plan | Optional, but recommended, key stage curriculum plan for each subject to check that continuity and progression can be achieved. Refer to PoS and LDs. | Subject groups. | End of year. |
| 5. Schemes of work | A scheme of work will be produced for each subject area that identifies specific learning objectives, resources, possible activities and assessment opportunities. Progression should be shown through the 6–10 weeks. | Year groups with subject co-ordinator advice. | Half-termly or termly. |
| 6. Lesson plans | Activities, groupings and differentiation. | Individuals. | Weekly. |

The above table reflects the advice given by SCAA (1995). SCAA identifies three key planning levels: long-term: key stage or year group plans; medium term: termly or half-termly plans; short-term: weekly or daily plans.

*Figure 2.5 Planning levels.*

## Key Stage Planning

Some subjects are more content-bound than others, so the creation of creating a key stage plan can be more easily done if the programmes of study for science, geography and history provide the framework for topic titles.

Figure 2.6 is an example of creating a key stage plan using this approach. The following steps are suggested:

1. Write out on cards the key statements of the science, geography and history programmes of study for key stage 1.
2. Bearing in mind the importance of revisiting topics (see Figure 1.6 – the spiral curriculum), duplicate elements as necessary.
3. Using a mixture of existing topic titles (to avoid reinventing the wheel) and new ones where necessary, put cards under titles to check that all the aspects can be covered.
4. Make decisions on the length of topics (this example goes for half-termly topics because of the age of the children and the desire to reflect the principles of the spiral curriculum). →

5. On a blank key stage matrix (Supplementary Material 1) organise the titles so that some progression is achieved through the key stage. Reference to the statements and level descriptions will help determine which topics are best suited to which year.
6. Write down the areas that will be ongoing on the right-hand edge of the plan.

In my experience, once a rough outline is achieved (no mean feat!) it is best to move on to the next level of planning (topic webs) and then return to the key stage plan to flesh out the detail. (Guidance for topic web planning can be found in Key Issues 3 in Chapter 1). Remember that this is the stage at which geographical *processes* of learning will be identified. The processes will then determine the focus of the topic and therefore the detail of the content to be selected.

## Curriculum Planning

The curriculum plan, an example of which is shown in Figure 2.7, shows which aspects of a topic will be taught in which week over a six-week period. (This period could be for four or ten weeks, or more.) The aim of a curriculum plan, as

| | Reception | Year 1 | Year 2 | Ongoing |
|---|---|---|---|---|
| **Autumn** | **Ourselves**<br><br>S | **Light & Sound**<br><br>S | **Living in the past**<br><br>H | e.g. weather records at various points during KS1 |
| | **Our toys**<br><br>H/G | **Leisure time**<br>Local area<br>H/G | **Places we play**<br>Local area<br>G | |
| **Spring** | **Home & School**<br>Local area<br>G | **Journeys**<br>Contrasting locality within the UK<br>G | **Communications**<br><br>H/G | |
| | **Old & New**<br><br>H | **Change & Growth**<br><br>S | **Living things**<br><br>S | |
| **Summer** | **Food**<br><br>S/G | **Packaging**<br><br>S/H/G | **Shops and shopping**<br>(mini topic because of end of key stage SATs)<br>G | |
| | **People who help us**<br>Local area<br>G | **Water**<br><br>S/G | **Hot & Cold**<br>Locality beyond UK<br>Castries, St. Lucia<br>S/G | |

*Figure 2.6 Whole school key stage 1 plan. S: Science; H: History; G: Geography. Where only one subject is shown, the topic has a single subject focus. Where more than one subject is shown, the topic has a multi-subject focus.*

for the key stage plan, is to ensure *continuity* and *progression*. The curriculum plan shown in Figure 2.7 covers the Year 2 topic "Places we play" listed in Figure 2.6.

### Continuity

*Continuity* refers to the experience that pupils have within and across key stages. This continuity of experience is determined by an agreed school policy on the nature of the subject, by providing similar teaching approaches and by building on previous experience. Within the National Curriculum for geography, the recurrent elements (Bennetts, 1995) which contribute to continuity are:

1. The study of places and themes.
2. The attention given to location and spatial pattern.
3. The studies focusing on the interaction between the physical and human elements of the environment.
4. The use of maps and the enquiry process.

### Progression

*Progression* refers to the progress which pupils make in their knowledge, understanding and skills. In geography progression is achieved through a gradual increase in: the breadth of study, including the variety of places and themes; the scale of study; and the depth of study, such as more powerful ideas and greater complexity of thought (both of which will be linked to the use of geographical vocabulary, see Figure 1.11).

Progression can only be achieved effectively when it is linked to assessment (see Section 3 below). It is therefore helpful to look at the level descriptions to identify what sort of progression across the key stage is envisaged. The paragraphs for each level can be separated to show three main strands: skills; knowledge and understanding; and environmental awareness. These strands and the progression within them can be seen in Figure 2.11.

## Schemes of Work

The curriculum plan is made up of subjects which are in turn made up of units of work. These units of work can be developed into schemes of work which identify *specific learning outcomes* for knowledge, understanding, skills and attitudes. A scheme of work will also identify:

1. The types of activities that are most appropriate for helping children to achieve these outcomes.
2. The resources which are necessary.
3. The links with the National Curriculum programme of study.
4. The assessment opportunities.

It is helpful to identify assessment opportunities at this stage so that these can be integrated into the planning process. Schemes of work can be developed by individual staff or by year teams, depending on the size of the school. If there is more than one class per year group, planning in teams is essential to ensure parity of experience.

Figure 2.8 uses the cube model to identify the three elements of skills, places and the environmental theme, before developing these ideas in more detail in the scheme of work, (see Figure 2.9). The topic (Water) is taken from the key stage plan shown in Figure 2.6

The topic web for water can be seen in Figure 1.8 (Key Issue 3 of Chapter 1).

| Topic: Places we play | | | | Year: 2 |
|---|---|---|---|---|
| Week | Geography | History | Science | Information Technology |
| 1 | Where do we play? Can these places be sorted into groups? | Where did I play when I was little? Are they the same as the places I play in now? Why? | | Branch program to sort lists of types of play areas. |
| 2 | Focus on outdoor play. Where are these places in our area? How do I get there? Mapping activities & use of large-scale OS map. | Where did my parents play as children? How can I find out? Devise questionnaire. | Why do we play? (Fun and exercise to keep healthy.) | Wordprocessing package to write questionnaire for history. |
| 3 | Focus on local playground. Fieldwork. What is there? Natural/manmade. What sort of play takes place? What is the ground covered with? Map area. | Process results – pictograms, bar charts, etc. Compare with own experiences. | Materials – different types and purposes. Safety. Forces and playground equipment. | Database program to process results of questionnaire. |
| 4 | Role-play 1. Developing a waste area into a park/playground. Look at points of view, e.g. grandparent, parent, child. | Send same questionnaire to grandparents. Do we expect the same results? | Design experiment to test strength of different materials. | Wordprocessing. |
| 5 | Role-play 2. Design and map park from your group's viewpoint. Are all maps the same? Why not? | Process results. Put all info. on a time-line plus pictures and descriptive writing, etc. Use reference books. | Consider results and relate again to uses. What other things apart from strength need to be taken into account? | Database "My World" package to design a play area. |
| 6 | Why do we have some types of play areas in our locality and not others? Distribution of larger centres, e.g. Alton Towers, leisure centres. | Interpret all results and consider questions relating to change and continuity, cause and effect. Play in distant past, e.g. Breughel painting. | | |

*Figure 2.7 Curriculum plan – this could be extended to include English, maths, art, RE and so on.*

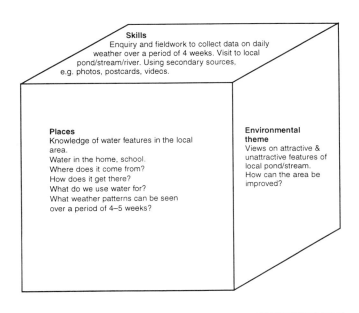

*Figure 2.8 Cube model for a topic on Water.*

The key things to remember when planning a scheme of work are:

1. Does the scheme reflect the requirements of the programme of study for key stage 1?
2. Does it give children the opportunity to achieve the types of learning that are reflected in the level descriptions?
3. Is progression evident through the scheme in terms of knowledge, understanding and skills? (A useful way of monitoring this is to check that the work in Week 1 prepares the way for work in Week 2 and that the work in Week 2 builds on the work in Week 1 and prepares the way for work in Week 3.)
4. Are the activities the most appropriate for developing the skills, knowledge or understanding identified?
5. Do the activities and learning outcomes relate directly to the key questions?
6. Is there a balance between learning outcomes and variety in types of activities planned?
7. Are assessment opportunities planned at relevant points during the scheme?
8. Has the use of IT been incorporated, where relevant?

An alternative way of approaching a scheme of work is to follow the enquiry route shown in Figure 1.10 in Chapter 1.

Further examples and blank matrices for INSET purposes can be found in Supplementary Material 2, 3 and 4.

To conclude, when planning a scheme of work for a locality study it is important for all staff to have an agreed definition of "the local area". This helps to ensure both consistency and continuity. Many schools will have already done a locality appraisal, but for those who have not (or who wish to review their definition) a locality appraisal sheet is provided in Supplementary Material 5.

## Cross-Curricular Dimensions and Themes

"A commitment to provide equal opportunities for all pupils and to prepare pupils for life in a multicultural society permeates the National Curriculum" (DES, 1991). This broad aim outlined in the non-statutory guidance of 1991 still applies to the revised Order of 1995. Geography is ideally placed to help children work towards the aims of multi-ethnic education. Through its focus on people and places, teachers can help to promote positive images, challenge stereotypes and present a balanced view. This applies equally to the consideration of male and female roles in different societies including our own.

The cross-curricular themes of education for the environment, citizenship and economic and industrial understanding seem to have declined in importance, judging by the lack of recent guidance from the DFE. However, they remain important elements of any curriculum and geography can make a significant contribution to their development. The environmental education theme can even be used to provide a framework for topic planning, within which there will be geographical, historical and scientific elements. Palmer (1994) builds many of her ideas around this approach to planning. She sees three interrelated components of environmental education:

1. Education *about* the environment – basic knowledge and understanding of the environment.
2. Education *for* the environment – values, attitudes and positive concern for the environment.
3. Education *in* or *through* the environment – using the environment as a resource with emphasis on enquiry, investigation and first-hand experiences.

It can be seen that the above are entirely in accord with some of the aims of geographical education. They can be effectively used to guide planning, particularly when the focus for a topic is linked to environmental geography or a particular issue: "The three components are inextricably linked, and are thus essential to the planning of educational programmes at all levels" (Palmer, 1994).

| Key questions | Learning outcomes | Activities (plus IT) | Resources | PoS |
|---|---|---|---|---|
| What is the weather today? (Ongoing) What water features can we name? | Develop geographical vocabulary associated with weather and water features. Extract info. from secondary sources. Notice similarities and differences. | Collect weather data daily. Use IT database to store info. Collect photos of lakes, sea, rivers, coast, etc. to sort and and discuss. | Weather board, thermometer, rain gauge, postcards and photos. | 1a 3a 3f |
| Where is the river? How do/did we get there? What is it like? What is it used for? Is it attractive or unattractive? | Be able to use a simple map to follow a route. Name physical and human features. Be able to roughly locate position on map. Record info. on tally chart. Make judgements about quality. | Visit local stream or river in small groups. Mark key features on pre-drawn map. Record types of river use on a tally chart. | Pre-drawn map to follow. Pot to collect sample of water. Record sheet. | 1b 2 3b 3d, e 5a 6a |
| Same questions as above. | Skills in use of symbols on own route maps. Describe features seen. Interpret data collected and draw conclusions. | Draw own maps of route taken and mark key features/landmarks using agreed symbols. Make pictograms using data collected. Discuss results. | Fieldwork data. | 3d 5d |
| What is a river? Where does it come from? Where does it go to? | Begin to understand that a river has a source, middle and flows into the sea. Use vocabulary of rivers and sequencing skills. | Watch video from "Watch" (BBC series) which shows a river from source to sea. Identify sequence stages in a river. Discuss. | "Watch" video. Three pictures of sequence + simple sentences. | 3a, f 5a |
| What is our weather like? Is it the same all year round? | Interpret data collected and secondary sources. Notice patterns in weather data collected. Use prior knowledge and secondary sources to predict whether the weather patterns will be the same at other times of the year. | Print off data collected from daily weather recordings. Teacher to ask questions to help children notice patterns. Have pictures of seasons. (Ask: Which season are we in?) | Database print-outs. | 3f 5c |

The scheme shows the first four weeks in detail. Further weeks would cover key questions such as: Where does the rain go when it falls on the ground? Where is water in the home and in school? What do we use this water for?

*Figure 2.9 Scheme of work for a topic on Water.*

## Section 3: Assessment and Key Stage 1 Geography

"Assessment is at the heart of the process of promoting children's learning" (TGAT, 1988). There is no statutory requirement to assess geographical learning through the use of Standard Assessment Tasks at the end of the key stages. The modes of assessment employed are therefore teacher assessment and pupil self-assessment (Mitchell and Koshy, 1993). The purpose of both types of assessment is twofold: to chart children's progress and to provide the basis for planning. Assessment is therefore an integral part of the planning process (see Figure 2.10). Two types of assessment can be identified: formative and summative.

### Formative Assessment

This is ongoing and helps to inform future planning for both individuals, groups of children and the whole class. It can be used at the beginning of a unit of work to assess children's previous knowledge, understanding and skills. It might also gauge attitudes that they hold regarding, for example, life in another locality.

### Summative Assessment

This provides a summary of achievement up to a particular point. This may be the end of a topic, year or key stage. At the end of a year or key stage its purpose is generally to inform others – the next class teacher, parents, government.

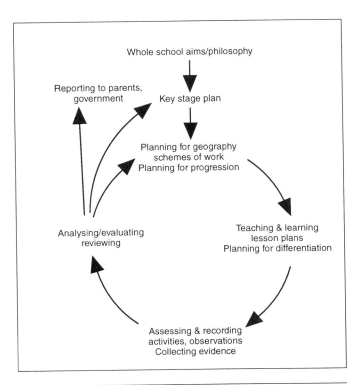

*Figure 2.10 The assessment and planning cycle.*

Preparing to assess children's learning in geography involves asking certain questions:

> 1. *What* to assess: Geographical knowledge (vocabulary, names of features, etc.), understanding (location, change, similarity and difference), skills (mapwork, enquiry and fieldwork) or attitudes (making judgements and seeing others' viewpoints)?
> 2. *How* to assess: Choose ways that are appropriate to assess geographical learning.
> 3. *Who* to assess: Individuals, groups, or the whole class?
> 4. *When* to assess: Before, during, or after a unit of work?

The first two will now be discussed in more detail.

## What to Assess

Assessment for formative purposes will depend partly on the stage of the topic at which the assessment is conducted. It will essentially take one of the following two forms:

> 1. Assessment of prior learning (knowledge, understanding, skills or attitudes) before beginning a new topic.
> 2. Assessment of recent learning at a point during a topic to ensure that the pupil/s is/are ready for the next step.

Reference to both the programme of study for key stage 1 and the level descriptions (LDs) is necessary when making decisions about what to assess. The LDs need to be examined in some detail if their meaning is to be made clear. Figure 2.11 shows the LDs broken up into the three main strands of skills, knowledge and understanding, and environmental awareness. This analysis makes it easier to identify progression through the levels, identify assessment objectives with greater clarity and aid planning.

When the terminology of the statements in Strand 2 is examined a broad pattern emerges which shows progression from knowledge to understanding and from Level 1 to Level 4.

### Knowledge

Level 1 typically involves observing, recognising and expressing views. Level 2 typically involves recognising, describing and selecting information.

### Understanding

Level 3 typically involves describing, comparing, and offering explanations. Level 4 typically involves describing, comparing, noticing geographical patterns, understanding geographical processes, and understanding causes and effects.

This reflects the two-tier questioning levels described in Key Issue 4 of Chapter 1.

Reference to subsequent levels, or Level 4 at least, is necessary because even if the level of understanding indicated is not assessed earlier, children will need to be working towards this type of understanding. This will also help to ensure continuity of experience across the key stages.

Level description statements and their terminology can then be applied to a specific topic in order to identify specific assessment criteria. These criteria provide the "yardstick" for assessment, the results of which could be used for either formative or summative purposes. Figure 2.12 below shows how this has been done for assessing knowledge and understanding of rivers within the Water topic.

Supplementary Materials 6 and 7 show how terminology can also be identified for the skills and environmental awareness strands. They leave room for applying what the levels say to developing assessment criteria as part of an INSET activity. Working as a staff on interpreting the level descriptions is essential if a common understanding of their meaning is to be reached and if they are going to be applied in a consistent way throughout the school.

| Progression in | Skills | Knowledge and understanding | Environmental awareness |
|---|---|---|---|
| Level 1 | Pupils use resources provided and their own observations to respond to questions about places. | Pupils recognise and make observations. | Pupils express their views on features of the environment of a locality that they find attractive or unattractive. |
| Level 2 | Pupils select information from resources provided. They use this information and their own observations to ask and respond to questions about places. They begin to use appropriate vocabulary. | Pupils describe physical and human features of places, recognising those features that give places their character. They show an awareness of places beyond their locality. | Pupils express views on attractive features of the environment, of a locality. |
| Level 3 | Pupils use skills and sources of evidence to respond to a range of geographical questions. | Pupils describe and make comparisons between the physical and human features of different localities. They offer explanations for the locations of some of those features. They show an awareness that different places may have both similar and different characteristics. They offer reasons for some of their observations about places. | Pupils offer reasons for some of their judgements about places. |

*Figure 2.11 Strands in the level descriptions.*

## How to Assess

It is not necessary for all teacher assessment to be formal. Primary teachers are very adept at making ongoing assessments of their children as they make informal observations on a daily basis. This type of assessment will obviously continue but there will be times when formal assessment is necessary, either by collecting and interpreting children's work or by using carefully structured assessment tasks.

*How* to assess cannot be separated from *what* to assess. The one will be determined to a large degree by the other. The key is clarity in identifying what to assess, and in devising assessment criteria that will serve as indicators of learning. Once this has been achieved, the next step is to choose the most appropriate assessment method that will enable children to demonstrate the skill, understanding or knowledge to be assessed. Types of assessment tasks need not differ from the range of activities that are appropriate for geographical study. The following provide some examples of how geographical learning might be assessed:

1. By interpreting maps – ask children to write a story based on the features shown in the map provided, describe what features they can see in the map and draw a picture of what they think this place might look like.
2. By drawing maps of routes, of imaginary places and of places described in a story.
3. By using photographs and pictures – ask the children to describe and name the features seen, label features in a picture, ask questions about what is shown, describe what the picture shows to another person who cannot see it, sort pictures into those showing physical and those showing human features. →

| Topic: Water | | Focus: Knowledge and understanding of water features, specifically rivers |
|---|---|---|
| Knowledge & understanding | Level 1: | Can recognise and name a river, the sea and a pond in a picture or out in the locality. Can talk about the feature. |
| | Level 2: | As above and can name the source and the mouth of a river in a picture. Can describe what a river is like. Knows that a river always flows to the sea. |
| | Level 3: | As above and can describe how a river changes from source to sea using picture clues. Can make comparisons between a river and another water feature (e.g. pond). Can give good reasons for some of the differences. |

*Figure 2.12 Using the level descriptions to identify assessment criteria for the topic on Water.*

4. By using geographical vocabulary – ask children to sort words into physical/human features, draw a picture to illustrate a word, and use the term correctly in a discussion.
5. By using geographical concepts – ask children to sort and describe similarities and differences, respond to teacher-led questions, and make decisions within the context of a role-play.

Examples of how to choose the most appropriate type of task are given below.

### Assessing Spatial Knowledge and Understanding

Research suggests that this means using something other than verbal recall or drawing a map for this purpose because young children's linguistic or motor skills are not sufficiently developed for them to be able to do themselves justice (see Key Issue 2 in Chapter 1). What does this mean in practice? Assessment has to be made of whether an understanding of the relative locations of, say, features in a street, has been achieved. The *assessment criterion* is: can children place features in the correct positions? (The number of features to place will depend on the age and ability of the children.) The *assessment task* is: ask children to place known features, represented by a selection of symbols, on a pre-drawn street map.

### Assessing Children's Knowledge About and Attitudes Towards a Distant Place

This has to be done before a study is embarked upon. There are no formal *assessment criteria* because this is assessing where the children "are at", and every child will hold different views. The *assessment task* is: The whole class, or small groups, should brainstorm a list of words that they associate with a place (e.g. India). A further list can be made after completion of the locality study (e.g. Chembakolli – see resources in Section 5) to see whether the images have changed. Alternatively, or in addition, children can be asked to draw a picture of the image the place brings to mind.

### Using Teacher-led Questions to Assess Knowledge and Understanding

The ability to ask questions that will actually assess what you want is an art in itself! Palmer (1994) gives some very helpful guidance. Figure 2.13 shows questions grouped in categories and the required thinking related to them. As mentioned in Key Issue 4 of Chapter 1, the knowledge questions should precede those that demand understanding. As Palmer (1994) states: "Questioning should not be left to chance. The effective teacher will plan for questioning in geography with the same rigour as for any other aspect of the early years teaching role."

| Category | Knowledge and understanding demonstrated | Teacher's questions |
|---|---|---|
| Knowledge | Recall of facts and basic understanding or observations (involving naming and describing). | 1. How wide was the playground?<br>2. What is the name of the river we saw?<br>3. What animals does the farmer have? |
| Comprehension | Comparing, contrasting, describing, explaining and interpreting facts. | 1. Can you explain why farmers grow food?<br>2. Which is higher – the river bank or the house on the hillside?<br>3. What type of animal does the farmer have most of? |
| Application | Applying knowledge to solve problems and classifying, selecting, and using information. | 1. Can you follow this plan to put the model village back in the right place?<br>2. Do all the world's people live in houses like ours? |
| Analysis | Drawing conclusions, making inferences, seeing patterns, finding causes, and using evidence. | 1. Why do you think people in the Arctic eat a lot of fish?<br>2. Why is water running down the side of the hill? |
| Synthesis | Solving problems, making predictions, proposing and generalising. | 1. What do you think would happen if the world got warmer and all the snow melted?<br>2. What do all schools need? |
| Evaluation | Judging, evaluating, deciding and appraising. | 1. Do you think it is a good idea to cut down trees in rain forests?<br>2. What would be the best use of this piece of wasteland? |

*Figure 2.13 Teachers' questions and the cognitive processes at key stage 1 (based on Palmer, 1994, Geography in the Early Years, p. 149, Routledge).*

## Collecting Evidence

The nature of many geographical tasks in the early years means that much of the work will be achieved through talk and action. Action may be sorting, sequencing, building models, arranging symbols on a base-map and so on. The most appropriate type of evidence is therefore likely to be photographic. Otherwise, if there is nothing tangible (drawings, writing, etc.), the most appropriate type of evidence will be teacher notes based on observations.

Figure 2.14 shows one possible way of recording such observations. It is designed for formative purposes, hence the Action column. The Possible Outcomes section is closely linked to the purpose of the activity and is discussed in more detail in Section 4 below. A blank matrix for recording teacher observations is provided in Supplementary Material 8.

The other main type of evidence will be that of children's work. This may be a drawing, a map, a chart, a list, a piece of writing or a combination of any of these. The SEAC (1993) materials give helpful guidance. SCAA has taken over the responsibility for publishing guidance on the application of level descriptions in geography.

## Section 4: Teaching Key Stage 1 Geography

"Effective learning cannot be left to chance. Children need to be engaged in structured and purposeful work which takes a diversity of forms" (Knight, 1993). Transforming a scheme of work into what children will actually be doing on a weekly basis is no easy task. For many, the most difficult part of the process is achieving progression from one session to the next, while at the same time trying to differentiate to

---

**Formative Teacher Assessment Record**

Name:                                          R ☐          Y1 ☐          Y2 ☐

Activity:                                       Date:

| Possible Outcomes | | |
|---|---|---|
| Why have I planned this activity? | | |

| Account | Interpretation | Action |
|---|---|---|
| What actually happened? | What does this tell me about the learner? | How does this help my next planning? |
| What did the child do, say, write or make? | What does the child know, understand or do? | What *might* I plan next? |

Comments: Any additional comments from the teacher, child or parents.

*Figure 2.14 Recording teachers' observations (Mitchell & Koshy, 1993).*

take account of the variety of abilities that there may be in the class. "This concept of match" (Bennett et al., 1984), which links with the concept of "fitness for purpose" (David et al., 1992), is examined with reference to specific examples of a series of lessons/activities.

The topics for which examples are given are all taken from the key stage plan outlined in Figure 2.6 (see Section 2). When planning these topics in more detail it is worth identifying where certain elements of the programme of study for key stage 1 recur. For example, Figure 2.15 shows the points at which locality studies (programme of study, point 6) are covered during key stage 1. Column 3 shows how locality work can be gradually built on and extended using the idea of the spiral curriculum shown in Figure 1.6 in Chapter 1.

Three examples of a series of activities are given below. These identify the types of geographical activity that might be undertaken and which parts of the programme of study they help children to meet. The first example is used to examine the issues of match and differentiation in depth.

### Example 1: Reception Topic: Home and School

Focus: The local area, early mapping skills, noticing similarities and differences.

Programme of study:
1. Investigate features of home and school.
2. Focus on geographical questions (see below).
3. Investigate home and school, observe, question, record and communicate ideas and information.  →

| Point during key stage | Topic | Areas revisited and built on | PoS |
|---|---|---|---|
| **Y2 Summer 2** | Hot & cold | Contrast locality beyond the UK – Castries, St. Lucia – using the GA photopack. As well as noting similarities and differences, work towards making comparisons, e.g. in Castries the roads have gutters like ours do, but they are much bigger because they have heavier rain. Link causes to effects. Interpret and get info. from different maps. | 1b, 1c 2 3d, 3e 3f 4 5a, 5b 5c |
| **Y2 Autumn 2** | Places we play | Further develop understanding of location and spatial distribution. Study physical features related to opportunities for play. Make plan of playground using symbols. | 1a, 1b 2 3a, 3b 3d, 4 5d, 6c |
| **Y1 Spring 1** | Journeys | Contrast locality within the UK: The Island of Coll, Scotland, based on *Katie Morag Delivers the Mail*. Study journeys, routes and transport networks. Spot similarities and differences in physical and human features and effects on people. Draw picture map of the place in the story, marking the route taken by Katie Morag. | 1b, 1c 2 3a, 3c 3d, 3e 3f 4 5a, 5b 5d |
| **Y1 Autumn 2** | Leisure time | What do we do in our spare time? What is there in the local area to provide for this? Add to understanding the character of the local area related to its size. Colour-code local area map. | 1a, 1b 3b, 3c 3d, 3f 4, 5a, 5d 6a, 6b |
| **R Summer 2** | People who help us | Study people in school and in the local area, locations of human features, e.g. school office, crossing point to school and doctor's surgery. Colour-code pre-drawn map. | 1a, 1b 3a, 3d 3f 4 5a, 5d |
| **R Spring 1** | Home & school | Identify similarities and differences in physical and human features. Ask how the two are connected, e.g. roads, paths, telephone lines, letters. Draw picture maps. | 1a, 1b 2 3a, 3b 3d, 4 5d |

*Figure 2.15 The spiral curriculum applied to locality studies throughout key stage 1.*

4. Undertake fieldwork activities at home and in school.
5. Make a plan of home/school with adult help.
6. Study a part of the locality of the school.
7. Look at similarities and differences between home and school.
8. Consider how these buildings are used.

Key questions (for home and school separately):
1. Where is this place?
2. What sort of place is it?
3. What are its main features?
4. What are the main activities that go on there?
5. How are the two places connected? (e.g. route from home to school/picture maps; telephone lines; letters and notes from school to home; and links between people).
6. What do you think and feel about this place?

Key questions (for comparison between home and school, focusing on rooms):
1. How are these places the same?
2. How are they different?
3. Which rooms do both places have?
4. Why might that be?
5. Are these rooms exactly the same? (How are they similar/different and why?)

As part of this topic, in order to help children achieve the understanding indicated in the comparison between the two places, the following provides a possible sequence of activities.

*Activity 1:* Send children home with a survey sheet, that they have helped to design, to complete with the help of an adult or older child. The children might design the sheet in these stages:

1. Make a list of all the types of rooms they have in their homes.
2. Discuss how they can record whether their home has these rooms (including possible use of symbols to help those who find reading hard).
3. Discuss and add details such as which room is the telephone in?

For an example of this survey sheet see Supplementary Material 16.

*Activity 2:* In groups, do a similar survey of the rooms that there are in school. Go through similar steps but this time discuss how the children can show, for example, the number of classrooms (tallying).

*Activity 3:* Collate and display information in various forms including tally chart, pictogram and bar chart.

*Activity 4:* Make a set of cards with pictures (drawn or cut out of magazines or using photographs) and labels for all the types of room both in home and school.

*Activity 5:* Using set circles, sort the pictures into rooms that a home has, rooms that a school has, rooms that both places have. Each group should do this in turn, with some adult input to encourage discussion and use of appropriate vocabulary. Display the results as a Venn diagram (see Figure 2.16).

*Activity 6:* Information could also be displayed in map form where two large-scale plans of a home and a school are provided, with those rooms that the two have in common colour-coded with a key. This could be done with a group of more able children, or made by the teacher for the class to look at and discuss.

*Activity 7:* Through carefully structured teacher-led questioning, help children to answer some of the questions above. Encourage them to look for patterns for themselves, for example, can they generalise from their observations:

1. What other buildings also have bedrooms?
2. Is there a type of room that all buildings will need, (e.g. a toilet)?

How does this example meet the idea of "fitness for purpose" (David et al., 1992)? The notion of fitness for purpose relates to making a match at two different levels. Firstly, there is the match that is necessary between the task and the objectives it is designed to meet, which is linked to the educational purpose of the task. Secondly, there is the

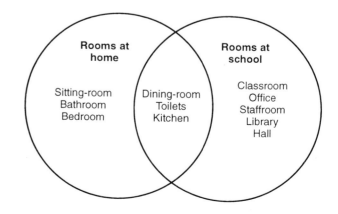

*Figure 2.16 Venn diagram to show rooms at home and school.*

match between the task and the child, which is all to do with differentiation.

*Match between Task and Purpose*

The overall purpose of the comparison between home and school is to encourage children to begin to look for things that are the same and things that are different about places. *Specific* learning outcomes for this series of activities might be:

*Knowledge*: Names of rooms at home and at school; know what the rooms are used for.

*Skills*: Enquiry – devise a survey sheet that will record what we want to find out. Collect information and process it for display. Represent information as a map. Answer geographical questions.

*Concepts*: Similarity and difference, cause and effect.

There are a number of ways of developing the above learning outcomes. The steps in Example 1, above, were chosen for the following reasons:

1. The children would be active in the learning process.
2. They would follow the enquiry route and record information in a way that is appropriate to geographical enquiry.
3. The sequence of activities is designed to enable the children to arrive at their own conclusions and hence develop the geographical concepts identified.
4. A variety of ways of grouping the children from whole class discussion through group to individual are used where appropriate.
5. The methods of recording and displaying information are geographical and are appropriate in terms of making it easier for the children to make comparisons. (Mapped information is usually a way of helping children to notice patterns in location but, in this case, it is used for familiarisation purposes.)
6. Questioning, as discussed in Chapter 1, is an appropriate way to encourage children to interpret the information collected and to make sense of it. This is the final activity in the sequence because it can be argued that knowledge needs to be established before understanding can be developed.

Point 4, above, mentions different ways of grouping children. "It is important for teachers to use a variety of teaching styles ranging from whole class, to group, to individual ... decisions about which ... make teaching young children a very complex task" (David et al., 1992). Groupwork, in particular, is demanding in terms of planning and organisation. Although most children are used to working *in* a group, the difficulty is to encourage them to work *as* a group. Working as a group, involving collaboration and sharing of ideas, is essential if the principle "what children can do collaboratively today they can do alone tomorrow" (Knight, 1993) is to be achieved.

Collaborative learning also reflects the idea discussed in Key Issue 2 of Chapter 1, that young children learn best through *action* and *talk*. Working as a group is one way of achieving that integration. Teacher's concerns about collaborative groupwork are often organisational:

1. Can I rely on the children to work as a group?
2. How will I know if they all took part?
3. How will I know if each child understood what he or she was doing?

There is no easy answer to this dilemma. Children will need to learn the skills of working as a group in the same way as any other. Many of the teaching approaches and methods described in Chapter One, Key Issue 4, are particularly well suited to this type of collaborative groupwork. Because of this, and because of the dividends for children in terms of more effective learning and working towards independence, it makes the effort of achieving effective groupwork worthwhile.

*Match between Task and Child – Differentiation*

"The programme of study for each key stage should be taught to all or the great majority of pupils in the key stage, in ways appropriate to their abilities" (DFE, 1995a). Matching the task to children's individual needs "is a very demanding professional skill" (CCW, 1991). Some children may be at the stage when they require practice (the introduction of a new skill or concept), while others may be at the stage when they need to apply the skill or concept to a new situation.

Children will also be coming from different starting points regarding their existing knowledge. Identification of these differences is intimately bound up with assessment (see Section 3, above) but there is also the problem of what to do about the differences once they have been identified. The new Geography Order recognises this in the statement: "Judgements made in relation to the level descriptions should allow for the provision (of individual needs) where appropriate" (DFE, 1995a). For example, when comparing home with school, are children being given the opportunity to do the following?

1. Recognise and make observations about features of places (Level 1).
2. Describe features of places and recognise which features give a place its character (Level 2).
3. Describe and make comparisons between features of different localities (Level 3).

Reference to level descriptions in this way will help to ensure that opportunities for achievement at different levels are being provided. Most teachers are fully aware of the range of abilities in their classroom and they differentiate their lessons in a variety of ways, sometimes without even consciously acknowledging that they are doing so. Planning differentiated tasks at a more conscious level will allow maximum participation by *all* pupils and thus meet the NCC requirement of equal access for all.

The three main types of differentiation are shown in Figure 2.17, and a model of the teacher as a "good differentiator" is shown in Figure 2.18. Example 1 above (Topic: Home and School) indicates the use of all three types of differentiation. Specifically, Activity 5 shows differentiation by task and by outcome.

*By task*, some groups sort pictures, some sort pictures and match name cards to them; some groups have more adult input than others.

*By outcome*: children with greater depth of understanding might note that a sitting-room and a staffroom have a similar purpose and therefore could be placed in the overlap section; some children might be able to justify their sorting more ably than others.

Previous NCC guidance on differentiation used the statements of attainment as indicators that could be used to check against planning. The new level descriptions do not give enough detail to be used in this way. Perhaps this is one of the reasons not to throw away the old Geography Order.

To conclude, if children are taught geography using the range of teaching methods suggested earlier (see Key Issue 4 in Chapter 1) this will often "free" them from the need to be literate and numerate. These methods will enable *all* children to develop a sense of place, an understanding of the inter-relationship between the physical and human landscape and an awareness of issues relating to environmental concern.

---

**Differentiation**

**By task**

1. Children study the same part of the PoS, but are given different tasks.
2. Children are set the same task, but some children have adult support or additional resources.
3. Children work in a group, but each child has a different role within the group.
4. Children have access to the same PoS, but groups are taught using different strategies.

**By outcome**

1. Children are involved in doing the same task from which a variety of results will be produced, indicating different levels of achievement.
2. The outcome is differentiated by the method of recording, e.g. drawing or writing.

**By a series of tasks**

1. Children undertake a series of structured tasks that become increasingly more complex.
2. Some children are expected to work through the tasks at a faster pace than others.

---

*Figure 2.17 How to differentiate.*

Two further examples are now given that show a series of lessons/activities. These could form the basis for some INSET where staff identify:

1. The matches made between task and outcome.
2. The types of differentiation indicated.
3. Which elements of the programme of study for key stage 1 are met.

## Example 2: Year 1 Topic: Journeys

Focus: A locality within the UK, in which the physical and/or human features *contrast* with those in the locality of the school.

Programme of study:
1. Compare the two localities.
2. Develop mapping skills.
3. Develop an understanding of similarity and difference, cause and effect.

Key Questions:
1. Where is Scotland?
2. Where is the Isle of Coll?
3. What sort of place is Coll?
4. What are its main features?
5. What are the main activities that go on there?
6. How is it connected to other places?
7. What do you think and feel about this place?

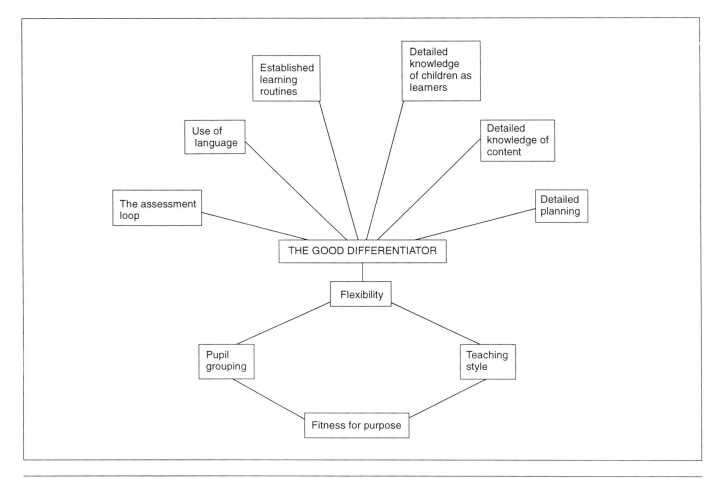

*Figure 2.18 The good differentiator.*

The following activities establish the character of Coll before comparing it with the children's own locality:

*Activity 1:* Read *Katie Morag Delivers the Mail* (see list of stories in Section 5). Discuss the place in the story – where might it be? Is it like the place in which the children live? On a globe and large map of the UK they could mark with a sticker where Coll is.

*Activity 2:* Have a simple pre-drawn map of Coll showing some of the features, but not the houses, mentioned in the story. Read the story again, following the route Katie took on the map. Groups could draw the relevant houses and indicate on the map where they think they go.

*Activity 3:* Write addresses for the letters and parcels. Perhaps a game, "Delivering the Mail", could be made up.

*Activity 4:* The children could draw their own map of the journey Katie took.

*Activity 5:* They could watch the BBC programme, *Words and Pictures*, that features the Isle of Coll. Groups could discuss and record what it is like to live on an island. What could they do, what couldn't they do? What are the advantages and disadvantages?

*Activity 6:* Draw pictures of what the island looks like and label with words discussed as a class, e.g. windy, rocky, small, sandy.

### Example 3: Year 2 Topic: Places We Play

Focus: The local area, understanding of the location and spatial distribution.

Programme of study:
1. How is the land used (the physical features and opportunities for play)?
2. How can the quality of the environment be improved?

Key questions:
1. Where do you play?
2. How do you get there?
3. Who goes/plays there?
4. Why do places need a play area?
5. Who decides what goes in a play area?
6. How do they make that decision?

The following activities relate to the role-play for planning a playground. (See also Supplementary Material 13 and 14.)

*Activity 1:* In groups the children could develop a character with reasons as to why s/he might use a park/playground and what sort of equipment s/he might therefore expect to find there. Each group could decide who will be the scribe and who will report back to the whole class.

*Activity 2:* Each group could work collaboratively to make a plan for their park/playground using the outline plan and symbols agreed as a class. They might like to do a draft plan first or use cut-out symbols on a base.

*Activity 3:* Display all the plans. The children could be asked: Are they the same? What is the same; what is different? Why are they different? There is only one place to put a playground, so what can we do?

## Section 5: Resources to Support Key Stage 1 Geography

OFSTED (1995) noted that the range of resources suitable for supporting primary geography had improved since the introduction of the National Curriculum in 1991, but that the availability of these resources in schools is still patchy.

The particular problem for early years teachers is that published materials are more often geared towards key stage 2 than key stage 1. What is available for key stage 1 is not always of good quality and is often very expensive (for example, some geography 'packs'). However, collecting and making up resource packs of your own, to support your children, school and community can be very time-consuming, even if more cost-effective.

The following section outlines a set of criteria upon which the suggestions for resources are based. These are *suggestions only* and are designed to give ideas with some concrete examples. No list of this type can be comprehensive.

## Criteria for Selecting Geography Resources

Various considerations need to be taken into account when building up resources to support geography teaching and learning.

1. Do the resources support the demands of the National Curriculum? PoS 2/3: Skills of mapwork, fieldwork and geographical enquiry; PoS 4: Places: local area; contrasting locality in and/or beyond the UK; PoS 5: Human and physical features and processes; PoS 6: Environmental issues; PoS 5/6: Concepts of location, cause and effect, patterns and processes, change and stability, similarity and difference.
2. Do the resources reflect the range of teaching approaches appropriate to geographical enquiry? Active, enquiry-based learning; Maps, globes, atlases, aerial photos etc.; Materials to support fieldwork; Resources for play and role-play; Pictures and photographs; Story books and non-fiction.
3. Do the resources reflect the needs of the school? The local area and the community; The ethnic mix of children; Special links the school has with the community and/or beyond.
4. Do the resources take account of special needs and the range of abilities in each year group?
5. Do the resources help counteract stereotypes of race, culture and gender and promote positive images of people and places?
6. Are there teacher resources to support both specialists and non-specialist teachers of geography?

## Resources for Mapwork

1. *Ordnance Survey maps* of local areas:
1:50 000 (2 cm:1 km) Landranger
1:25 000 (4 cm:1 km) Pathfinder, Outdoor Leisure or Explorer
1:10 000 (1 cm:100 m) Shows contours, good for street patterns.
1:2500 (1 cm:25 m) Plan style, very detailed.
1:1250 (1 cm:12.5 m) Only available for large urban areas.
Available from: Education Team, Room C454, Ordnance Survey, Romsey Road, Southampton SO16 4GU (Tel: 01703 792960/ 792795).

2. *Aerial photographs* (overhead and oblique) of the local area to match scale of OS 1:2500; of other places; human and physical landscapes. Available from:
The GOAD Map Shop, 8–12 Salisbury Square, Old Hatfield, Herts AL9 5BJ (Tel: 01707 271171).

National Remote Sensing Centre Ltd (formerly GEONEX), Education Department, NRSC Airphoto Group, Arthur Street, Barwell, Leicestershire LE9 8GZ (Tel: 01455 844513).
Photo Air, Photo Air House, 191A Main Street Yaxley, Peterborough PE7 3LD (Tel: 01733 241850).
A cheap alternative here are the seven photographs that accompany the SEAC key stage 1 SAT materials (1993).

3. *Satellite images* are now available in cheaper forms and can be useful for identifying land/sea, large urban areas and large physical features such as lakes and mountains. *Images of Earth : A teacher's guide to remote sensing at Key Stage 2* was published by the Geographical Association in 1992. It is a 96 page book, with 21 A4 images (colour and black and white) and three full colour posters. Although designed for key stage 2, the satellite images may be useful for key stage 1.
Other satellite images are available from:
Map Marketing Ltd 92–104 Carnwath Road, London SW6 3HW (Tel: 0171 736 0297). They also stock poster size images of London and the Home Counties, Europe and the Earth.

4. *Miscellaneous sources:* The above range of maps and aerial views can be quite expensive. To supplement these and broaden the variety available the following can be collected either free or for very little charge: estate agent's maps, road sign maps, postcard maps, bus maps, maps in adverts, underground maps, housing estate maps, storybook maps, tourist leaflets, guidebook maps, rail maps, children's maps, board game maps, playmat road layouts, road maps/atlases, playmat farms, etc., town centre maps and Lego road layouts.

5. *Globes:* as well as the conventional physical and political globes there are now a range of inflatable globes available. They are in different sizes and all have an attachment by which they can be hung from a ceiling and are very user-friendly for key stage 1 children. Available from:
Cambridge Publishing Services, P.O. Box 62, Cambridge CB3 9NA.

6. Another useful resource is the range of plastic, *table-top sized map outlines* of the UK, Europe and the World. These are coloured in bright green for the land and bright blue for sea. They are good for country and land/sea recognition, as well as for use as backdrops for weather forecasts. Available from:
MJP GEOPACKS, Freepost 23, St. Just, Penzance, Cornwall TR19 7JS (Tel: 01736 787808).

7. *Atlases:* there is a need to evaluate these quite carefully before buying. Often atlases for key stage 1 have been simplified to such an extent that the images portrayed can be stereotypical and present an unbalanced view of the world. Publishers of atlases suitable for key stage 1 include Hamlyn, Schofield and Sims, Usborne and Phillips.

8. Published schemes for supporting the development of *map skills* such as:
Collins Longman: *Mapstart* (revised, 1993), Simon Catling.
Scholastic: *Starting Geography "Mapping Skills"* (1993) has 56 photocopiable sheets.
NES Arnold: *Teaching Geography Maps in the National Curriculum Key Stage 1/2* (1992).

## Resources for Fieldwork

1. *Camera:* this is essential for recording features and gradually building up a bank of useful photographs of your local area.

2. *Equipment:* simple weather instruments (rain gauge, giant thermometer, etc.) Available from:
Hope Education, Orb Mill, Huddersfield Road, Oldham, Lancs OL4 2ST (Tel: 0161 633 6611).

Also useful are clip boards, counters for counting things like traffic, a stopwatch and sample/specimen bags or boxes. Many of the resources used to support science fieldwork will probably suffice.

## Play Equipment

The Royal Society for the Prevention of Accidents, Safe and Sound role-play equipment is useful for road safety, but also helps children to identify roads, pavements and kerbs and introduces appropriate vocabulary. Available from:
RoSPA, Cannon House, The Priory, Queensway, Birmingham B4 6BS (Tel: 0121 200 2461).

Hope Education (see above) supplies a variety of play equipment that can be used to support geography. Examples of its stock are: play cans and food packs for home corner role-play, place settings, roadway and farmyard floor puzzles, and road, countryside and town playmats.

## Pictures and Photographs

Time is well spent making a collection of photographs of your own local area and developing them to A5 or A4 size. If you are concerned that this expense is unwarranted because they will be spoiled through handling, make a set of colour photocopies mounted on card and covered in sticky-back plastic or laminate. The collection can then be added to year by year. (See also Section 4 of Chapter 3 for suggestions on Photo-CD technology).

Apart from your own collections of local photographs, postcards, pictures from tourist brochures and so on, there is an increasing number of photopacks on the market that are designed to meet the requirements of distant place study in the National Curriculum. The following examples are designed for key stage 2 unless specified. The activity suggestions may therefore be inappropriate but the photographs themselves are still an excellent resource and, as the packs vary in price from about £10.00 to £15.00 they are well worth the money. Available from:

ACTIONAID, The Old Church House, Church Steps, Frome, Somerset BA11 1PL.

The Geographical Association, 343 Fulwood Road, Sheffield SI0 3BP (Tel: 0114 2670666) publishes:
*Focus on Castries St. Lucia* photopack;
*Kaptalamwa (KS1/2): A Village in Kenya*;
*Ladakh Photopack*: an activity-based pack focused on the life of a Tibetan Community;
*Discovering Distant Places (KS1/2)* – a booklet to give guidance on using photopacks;
*Flatford: A contrasting UK locality (KS1/2)*

Available from World Aware, Catton Street, London WC1R 4AB (Tel: 0171 834 3844) are:
*Adokorpe: A Village in Ghana*;
*My Village Ilesha: Nigeria*;
*Where Camels are better than Cars: a small town in Mali*

Available from World Wildlife Fund, Panda House, Weyside Park, Godalming GU7 1XR:
*A Tale of Two Cities: Calcutta, India, and London, UK.*

## Storybooks for Geography Teaching

As discussed in Key Issue 4 of Chapter 1, stories provide an invaluable resource for teaching geography. Many stories have a strong sense of place, some focus on people and the way they live, while others are concerned with environmental issues. Stories can act as a stimulus for mapwork and help to develop the vocabulary of physical and human features.

### Story Books for Geography

In addition to classic stories such as "Goldilocks and the Three Bears", "Little Red Riding Hood" and "The Three Little Pigs", the following contemporary stories can also support geography teaching:

Aardema, V. (1986) *Bringing the Rain to Kapiti Plain*, Macmillan.

Ahlberg, A. and Wright, J. (1980) *Mrs Plug the Plumber*, Penguin.

Andrews, J. (1985) *Eva's Ice Adventure*, Methuen.

Anello, C. and Thompson, S. (1989) *The Farmyard Cat*, Hodder & Stoughton.

Anholt and Anholt (1995) *All About You*, Heinemann.

Armitage, R. and Armitage, D. (1977) *The Lighthouse Keeper's Lunch*, André Deutsch.

Baker, J. (1989) *Window* and *Where the Forest Meets the Sea*, Walker Books.

Brown, R. (1991) *The World That Jack Built*, Red Fox.

Cowcher, H. (1993) *Antarctica*, Picture Corgi.

Dahl, R. (1995) *Fantastic Mr. Fox*, Puffin Story Books.

Dahl, R. (1987) *The Enormous Crocodile*, Picture Puffin.

Daly, N. (1994) *Not So Fast Songololo*, Picture Puffin.

dePoala, T. (1990) *Bill and Peter Go Down the Nile*, Oxford University Press.

Dupasquier, P. (1986) *Dear Daddy*, Penguin.

Flindall, J. (1990) *Journey Home*, Walker Books.

Foreman, M. (1988) *Dinosaurs and All That Rubbish*, Picture Puffin.

Ganley, H. (1986) *Jyoti's Journey*, André Deutsch.

Gray, N. And Ray, J. (1995) *A Balloon for Grandad*, Orchard Books.

Grifalconi, A. (1989) *The Village of Round and Square Houses*, Macmillan.

Hedderwick, M. (1989) *Katie Morag and the Tiresome Ted*, Picture Lions.

Hedderwick, M. (1992) *Katie Morag Delivers the Mail*, Picture Lions.

Hedderwick, M. (1994) *Peedie Pebbles Summer/Winter Book*, Bodley Head.

Hughes, S. (1993) *Dogger*, Red Fox.

Hutchins, P. (1994) *Rosie's Walk*, Picture Puffin.

Hutchins, P. (1994) *Don't Forget the Bacon*, Picture Puffin.

James, S. (1991) *Dear Greenpeace*, Walker Books.

Mennen, I. and Daly, N. (1990) *Somewhere in Africa*, Bodley Head.

Milne, A. A. (1978) *Winnie the Pooh*, Magnet.

Orr, K (1990) *My Grandpa and the Sea*, Carolrhoda Books Inc., Minneapolis, USA.

Pienowski, J. (1988) *Weather*, Heinemann.

Rosen, M. (1989) *We're Going on a Bear Hunt*, Walker Books

Taylor, L. and Langley, J. (1994) *A Pig Called Shrimp*, Sainsbury's & Harper Collins.

## Other Useful Sources of Learning Materials

1. SEAC (1993) Children's Work Assessed at key stage 1: *Geography and History*, plus the Teacher's Pack of Standard Assessment Tasks for key stage 1 remains a useful resource. It has photocopiable materials on mapwork, the weather, the local area and people and work. There are also seven photographs, some of them aerial, showing: the Scilly Isles: a coastal scene; Montgomery, Powys: a village; Flatford Mill, Suffolk: river and countryside; Conwy, Gwynedd: town, castle and coast; Stockport, Cheshire: an urban scene; Greenland: a snow scene; and Niger: a desert village.

2. The Geographical Association (see address given above) produces an excellent quarterly journal *Primary Geographer*, as well as a range of other resources suitable for key stage 1. The Association publishes catalogues regularly.

3. Development Education Centres (DECs) produce materials that support the development of attitudes and values, particularly towards issues relating to the interdependent nature of our world and the environment. Birmingham DEC has the largest range of materials suited to the lower primary age-range. As well as booklets with helpful and practical teaching ideas, there are photopacks, games and simulations all available from:
Birmingham Development Education Centre, Gillett Centre, 998 Bristol Road, Selly Oak, Birmingham B29 6LE (Centre for all DECs).

4. BBC Education: Chief Education Officer, Room 2300, BBC White City, 201 Wood Lane, London W12 7TS.

5. Finally, a number of schemes have been published in recent years to support key stage 1 geography by Heinemann, Ginn and Collins. These will continue to be useful resources and are likely to be updated to accommodate the 1995 Geography Order.

# Chapter 3: The Role of Information Technology in Early Years Geography

## Section 1: Information Technology and the National Curriculum

"Information technology may be defined as the technology associated with the handling of information: its storage, processing and transmission in a variety of forms by electronic means, and its use in controlling the operation of machines and other devices" (DES, 1989). When asked to define information technology, a common first response from teachers is that it is to do with using computers in the classroom. In Nursery, Infant and First Schools this is often accompanied by discussion of the limitations of computers in early years classrooms. These limitations are often tied to a lack of time and/or resources to use the computer effectively, and to various technical problems. These issues will be discussed more fully in Section 2 below. Information technology (IT) is, however, very user-friendly and extremely accessible for early years teachers. Teachers need not be put off by the rhetoric. There are many ways in which IT can be incorporated into geographical work in an appropriate way.

The secret is to start simply and to move on from there. Remember that: "IT, with its speed, power and versatility, offers a unique resource in teaching and learning." (Koshy & Dodds, 1995). A simpler definition of IT is given by Anita Straker (1989): "Information technology, or IT, is the name which is given to machines which process information". Examples of such machines are video and audio recorders, telephones, calculators, cash tills, electronic weighing scales, library catalogue systems, fax machines, Ceefax and computers. Computers are also used to control devices such as traffic lights, automatic doors, washing machines, central heating systems and other everyday devices. The control of these devices will involve programming in some form or another.

There is therefore much more to information technology than computers. This chapter will consider children's IT capability in its fullest sense in order to broaden the perception of the range of opportunities that are both available and appropriate for the development of IT in the early years. More specifically, this will be related to the role IT has in supporting children's learning in geography.

## IT in the National Curriculum

The status of IT in the new National Curriculum is that of a *core skill*. The fact that the DFE has produced a separate document, *Information Technology in the National Curriculum* (DFE, 1995b) reflects this rise in status from earlier years. The geography document states that all schools should give pupils: "opportunities, where appropriate, to develop and apply their information technology (IT) capability in their study of geography" (DFE, 1995a). It is up to individual schools and teachers to determine where and when these opportunities arise, but geography provides an ideal context for much IT work, "particularly in supporting an enquiry-based approach to the subject" (Russell, 1995).

At key stage 1 the focus statement for IT states: "pupils should be taught to use equipment and software confidently and purposefully to communicate and handle information, and to support their problem-solving, recording and expressive work" (DFE, 1995b). At the same time, under key stage 1 skills, the geography document states that pupils should be taught to "use secondary sources, e.g. ... photographs (including aerial photographs)... CD-ROM encyclopaedia, to obtain geographical information" (DFE 1995a).

CD-based technologies in particular are a rapidly expanding area and are often under-exploited at key stage 1. Examples of how they can be used with young children are given in Section 3 below. As IT is perceived as an area that continues to require whole school and staff development, guidance is being produced for each of the National Curriculum subjects. Guidance for primary geography is already available. A concertina leaflet, *Primary Geography: a pupil's entitlement to IT*, has been published by The Geographical Association in conjunction with the National Council for Educational Technology (GA/NCET, 1995). Free copies are available from either of the above organisations (the addresses are given in Section 4 below). The leaflet contains practical advice and information which will help geography co-ordinators and classroom teachers to develop policy, planning and practice.

## Section 2: Current Practice in Early Years Information Technology and Geography

In order to suggest realistic activities in geography that can involve the use of IT, it was considered appropriate to identify present practice in the early years. A piece of small-scale research was conducted in some primary schools in two LEAs, the results of which are discussed below.

The research was conducted using an interview schedule with 12 teachers in 7 schools (see Figure 3.1). The aim was not to identify the best of practice, but to ascertain what is *common practice*. Schools were therefore not selected for anything other than a willingness to take part in the research. The discussion acknowledges that the sample was very small and can therefore only give limited insight into present practice.

The interview schedule included questions relating to the following issues:

1. The type of IT hardware.
2. The computer program used to support geography.
3. The non-computer use of IT to support geography study.
4. How IT is planned in schools.
5. How schools keep pace with advances in IT.

Each of these will now be dealt with in turn.

### Type of Hardware

In general schools have one computer per class. The types of computer used are Acorn (Archimedes family), BBC and Nimbus. The most popular are Acorn (Archimedes) and BBC. The reasons for this include the fact that Acorns are available on special offer through a supermarket promotion and BBCs were bought during the 1980s under the government funding scheme. In many cases, BBCs were gradually replaced by Nimbus computers, but priority for these tends to be given to Years 3–6.

Other hardware includes both colour and black and white printers to which most classes had access but which (reportedly) often broke down. Several classes had concept keyboards. One school also had a CD-ROM player and a Lego Control Centre. All schools had access to between two and four programmable 'toys' such as "Pip" and "Roamer".

### Computer Programs Used to Support Geography

The following programs (with examples in brackets) were named as familiar to teachers:

1. Data Handling ("Our Facts").
2. Wordprocessing ("Folio", "Write-on", "Podd", and "Phases").
3. Logo programming ("Tiny Logo", "Roamer", "Pip" and "Mazes").
4. Modelling ("My World" and "Our School").
5. Graphics ("Paintspa" and "Easel").
6. Adventures and Games ("Blob", "Animated Numbers", "Animated Alphabet", "Albert's House", "Little Red Riding Hood", "Granny's Garden" and "Teddy Bears' Picnic").

| | Type of school | Nursery | Reception | Y1 | Y2 | IT support teacher | Total |
|---|---|---|---|---|---|---|---|
| S1 | Primary | | ✔ | ✔ | ✔ | | 3 |
| S2 | Infant & Nursery | ✔ | | | | ✔ | 2 |
| S3 | Infant & Nursery | ✔ | ✔ | | | | 2 |
| S4 | Primary | | | | ✔ | ✔ | 2 |
| S5 | First & Middle Combined | | ✔ | | | | 1 |
| S6 | Infant & Nursery | | ✔ | | | | 1 |
| S7 | Primary | | | ✔ | | | 1 |
| | Total | 2 | 4 | 2 | 2 | 2 | 12 |

*Figure 3.1 Schools and teachers interviewed.*

Of these, the types of programs used most frequently were modelling, wordprocessing, programmable toys and computer games. The latter was by far the most popular. Most teachers saw IT having a role in developing mapwork skills and, more specifically, the use of directional and positional vocabulary.

Teachers were asked what geography work was currently being undertaken and whether this involved the use of IT. Responses showed that all classes had a geographical element to their current topic. Examples of these were habitats, farm locality, homes, contrasting locality, local shops, weather and journeys. All of these involved some fieldwork and mapping. Some classes also made use of photographs and model-making. However, in three of the seven schools, none of this work involved the use of IT. In schools which were using IT in their current work, they used "Pip" or "Roamer" to develop and reinforce mapping skills and "Our School" simulation and "Our Facts" to record weather data.

## Non-Computer Use of IT to Support Geography

In general IT work was perceived to be computer-based. Some teachers mentioned other types of IT work such as:

1. Tape-recording impressions of a journey.
2. Role-play in the home corner after a visit to a supermarket that included use of a cash-till and the pretence of "swiping" the items across the bar-code.
3. Pre-IT work in a Reception class that involved data-handling without the computer.

## How IT is Planned in Schools

The main finding was that although non-computer-based work would be planned as an integral part of the topic, computer use tended to be a "bolt-on" extra.

Most teachers had children using the computer every day, but this was rarely to support geographical work. In Nursery and Reception classes the priority was to familiarise children with the computer and to use programs that were linked to work in English or maths. Sometimes these programs had an incidental link with positional vocabulary through the movement of the cursor up, down or sideways.

In Year 1 and Year 2 classes more 'geographical' programs were used. These were generally chosen because they had some link with the topic title, for example, "My World" during a topic on the local area. Teachers working in Year 1

and Year 2 also chose more open-ended software, such as wordprocessing or data-handling programs. The use of these programs was more integrated for example: "Our Facts" to handle weather data; "My World" to deal with maps and weather charts; and " Phases" to write up weather reports.

The overall pattern was that computer-based work was not an integral part of the main planning process. Typically, it was something done in addition to the main work, and was rarely followed up. Teachers stated this was mainly because of time pressures and because other areas of the curriculum were perceived to be of greater importance.

## How Schools Keep Pace with Advances in IT

Keeping up to date was seen to be a big problem. Both LEAs in this survey had adviser support and all the schools which were interviewed had a member of staff who was responsible for IT development. However, teachers identified a number of factors which contributed to training being less effective that it might be:

1. Lack of confidence: if training is not put into practice straight away, or technical problems are experienced, this quickly undermines the effectiveness of training.
2. Lack of time: training may have been provided in certain types of programs but it is difficult to keep up with all the new ones as they become available.
3. Lack of suitable programs: this was seen as a real problem for the early years; most geographical programs are for older pupils and key stage 1 material is not always of good quality.
4. Using old equipment: key stage 1 classes were often at the bottom of the list when it came to financing new hardware and software.

## Discussion of Results and Implications for Practice

The patterns in practice that emerged from the research fall into five categories:

*Category 1:* Teachers mostly felt confident in their ability to teach geography and this confidence had grown since the implementation of the earlier National Curriculum in 1991. However, they were less confident in IT and particularly in perceiving a role for IT in geography. It is interesting that, when asked "Does IT have a role in early years geography teaching?" most teachers said, "Yes", but many also said that, before the interview, they would have been hard pressed to see the relevance of IT in geography. As the interview progressed, some teachers realised that elements of their IT work was geographical, even if incidentally through directional vocabulary associated with moving the cursor keys.

*Category 2:* Perception of IT work centres around the use of the computer and control devices such as "Pip" or "Roamer". Very few teachers mentioned the use of other IT tools, such as video or audio-cassettes. This was not because they were not used but because they were not perceived as being part of IT.

*Category 3:* The application of IT in all subjects, including geography, increases from Nursery and Reception to Year 2. IT was a lower priority with younger children (as was geography in some cases) because, for this age-group, the teachers' main concern was to teach the core subjects, art and craft, and socialisation skills.

*Category 4:* The *types* of program used changed from Nursery to Year 2 (see Figure 3.2). This move from "drill" and closed programs to more open-ended programs was seen as a necessary progression in the children's ability to use IT. It also has a fairly profound effect on the nature of the role of IT in geography teaching and learning.

| Nursery: | Computer games and pre-computer skills. Computers used daily by individual or groups of pupils by choice in the classroom. |
| --- | --- |
| Reception: | Computer games, drawing/designing programs, occasionally wordprocessing and rarely databases. Computer more often used weekly by individuals or groups, by choice and directed by the teacher, in the classroom. |
| Y1/Y2: | Full range of programs used at one time or another. Wordprocessing and games on a weekly basis, "Pip" "Roamer" and databases used occasionally. Individuals use the computer more often than groups, by choice and directed by the teacher, in the classroom. |

*Figure 3.2 Pattern of computer use in the early years.*

*Category 5:* For all teachers *time* was a major consideration when planning the use of IT tools of any kind. With younger children adult input is frequently needed if effective learning is to take place. Children in this age-group are also less able to cope if technical problems are experienced.

The implications of this research are now addressed, using the same five categories identified above:

1. Raise awareness of the relevance of the geographical elements to IT work already being carried out. Build on this and formalise it at the planning stage.
2. Extend awareness of the range of IT opportunities to include non-computer-based IT work.
3 & 4. Build on what teachers already know is good practice in terms of progression in IT capability. For example, one Nursery teacher thought the fact that many of the programs she used were closed in nature was an advantage. It gave children the opportunity to practice in a safe and controlled situation. They had a sense of achievement and enjoyed the repetitive element, rather as they like listening to a favourite story or doing a favourite puzzle again and again. This reflects the principle of the spiral curriculum that familiar activities which consolidate learning are just as important as those which are more exploratory and stretching.
5. Realise that there is a real need for suggestions to be practical, easy to implement and realistic given the time/organisational constraints operating in early years classrooms.

The following section will look at the application of IT in geography taking the above points into account.

## Section 3: Planning and Using Information Technology in Early Years Geography

This section begins by considering some principles in the planning of IT in geography. It then moves on to suggest some activities under two headings: non-computer-based IT and computer-based IT. Because the role of IT in early years geography is almost a whole book in itself, suggestions for activities will only focus on one or two key ideas.

When developing principles for the role of IT in geography, the whole can be summed up by the following question: "How can IT help children learn geography?" Essentially this entails reflecting on what it is that geography is all about and then considering whether IT has a role there. The leaflet produced by the Geographical Association and the National Council for Educational Technology (see Figure 3.3) provides an excellent framework for this.

Other principles might reflect the following questions (adapted from Straker, 1989):

| How can IT help pupils' learning in geography? | When undertaking geographical activities pupils will: | IT can enhance this activity by: |
|---|---|---|
| 1. By enhancing their skills of geographical enquiry. | Ask geographical questions. Observe, record and investigate data from fieldwork and secondary sources. Create, use and interpret maps at a variety of scales. Communicate and present findings. | The use of: Databases, spreadsheets, or data logging equipment, e.g. for a study of shopping, farming or the weather. Software to present information in a variety of ways, e.g. text, graphs and pictures. Concept keyboards to investigate images of localities and develop map skills. |
| 2. By providing a range of information sources to enhance their geographical knowledge. | Draw on appropriate sources to obtain information, ideas and stimuli relating to places and geographical themes. Become familiar with and use geographical vocabulary. | Providing access to: People and first-hand data using electronic mail (e-mail) and fax. Photograph, video, sound and other information, e.g. on CD-ROM, to study another locality or environment. |
| 3. By supporting the development of their understanding of geographical patterns and relationships. | Recognise patterns, and make comparisons between places and events. | The use of: Databases and spreadsheets, simulations and multimedia to provide an insight into geographical relationships, e.g. weather patterns, changes in traffic flow, or causes and effects of water pollution. A floor turtle to develop spatial awareness. |
| 4. By providing access to images of people, places and environments. | Develop an awareness and knowledge of the culture and character of places. | Providing access to: People and first-hand data using e-mail and fax. TV, photographs, video, sound and other information, e.g. on CD-ROM, to study another locality or environment. |
| 5. By contributing to pupils' awareness of the impact of IT on the changing world. | Use specific examples to illustrate how IT influences communication, leisure and the world of work. | Creating opportunities to discuss how computers are used to: Book a holiday. Control stock in supermarkets. Transmit information via satellite communications. Forecast the weather. |

*Figure 3.3 How IT can help pupils learn geography (The Geographical Association NCET, 1995).*

1. Has planning incorporated progression from Nursery/Reception through to Year 2?
2. Will the children do and learn things that are worth doing and learning?
3. Is using IT the most effective way of doing and learning these things?
4. Are there gender issues that need to be considered, for example, when planning individual and group use of computers?
5. Is IT an integral part of planning at *all* levels, from the whole school to individual classes?

At whole school and year group levels this will mean having an IT strand to planning documents such as the Key Stage Plan and the Scheme of Work. At classroom level, similar principles apply to the planning of IT as to the planning of fieldwork (see Key Issue 4 of Chapter 1). See Figure 3.4 for a planning cycle for information technology.

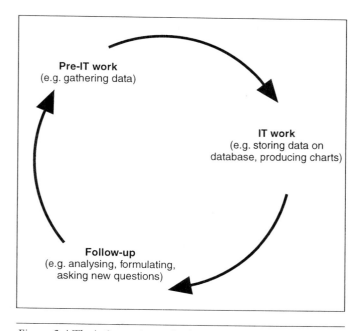

*Figure 3.4 The information technology planning cycle.*

A blank matrix for planning geography IT activities is provided in Supplementary Material 9.

## Non-Computer-Based IT in Geography

Non-computer-based IT means any IT work that does not involve children sitting at a computer or using "Pip" or "Roamer". This section focuses on developing an awareness of the impact of IT, including computer control technology, on the world and our everyday lives.

A key focus for work with young children will be on the term *information* technology. There is a need for children to develop an understanding of what information is before they can begin to understand how it has been affected by technology. Some key questions that might help children develop this understanding are:

1. What is information?
2. What types of information are there?
3. What does information look like?
4. How do we get information?
5. Where do we go for information?
6. How can we select information?

If enquiry is central to geography teaching and learning (see Key Issue 4 of Chapter 1) then consideration of these questions may already be an integral part of the topic being studied. They will be particularly appropriate when the topic is one which relies more on the use of secondary sources. For example, when studying a distant locality, the following activities might be planned:

1. Make a collection of the variety of different types of geographical information.
2. Ask children to sort, select, group or classify this information (early information-handling skills).
3. Make a display of the different types of information. Link this to a display of pictures/key words showing where this information comes from.

A similar set of questions could be applied to technology:

1. What is technology?
2. How does technology help us to store and find information?
3. In what ways does computer technology affect our daily lives?

Such questions could be applied to a topic on the world of work with information collected and displayed in the same way as above.

Figure 3.5 gives further examples of non-computer-based IT activities that can help meet the five basic objectives outlined in Figure 3.3.

| How can non-computer based IT help pupils' learning in geography? | Examples of activities which might contribute to a pupil's entitlement to IT in geography |
|---|---|
| 1. By enhancing their skills of geographical enquiry. | Undergo an investigation of ways in which computers are used to control the environment outside and in the home. This might be linked to a topic on people's jobs and what makes them easier, e.g. the librarian and computerised catalogue systems; the home carer and washing machine programmes. |
| 2. By using a range of information to develop geographical knowledge. | As part of a contrasting UK locality study, fax the link school (if you have one) with information about your locality and request similar imformation in return. Fax both text and pictures. |
| 3. By developing an understanding of geographical patterns and relationships. | As part of a topic on transport, video record traffic passing a chosen spot, e.g. at 10 a.m. and 1 p.m. every day for five days. Have the camcorder on for 2 mins each time. Watch results and see if a pattern emerges as to the busiest time of the day or week. What prediction could be made about the weekend? |
| 4. By experiencing images of people, places and environments. | For a contrasting locality study beyond the UK, use info. from video, photographs, satellite images, music recordings and other sources to help build up a picture of what sort of place it is. Compare with similar sources of own locality. |
| 5. By increasing awareness of the impact of IT on the changing world. | Pupils talk about different technologies in the home. They create a wall display of pictures of machines. They sort them into those that can and those that cannot be controlled. |

*Figure 3.5 Examples of non-computer-based activities.*

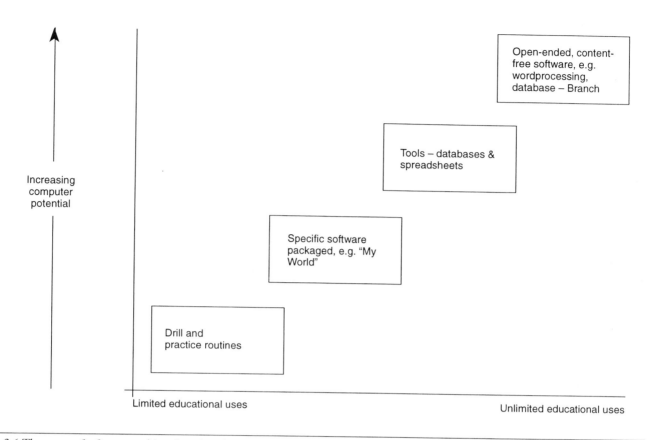

Figure 3.6 *The range of software and its educational uses (adapted from Bowden, 1991).*

(A further non-computer-based activity can be found in Supplementary Material 12. It is an example of developing pre-computer skills in handling data, linked to a topic on the weather.)

## Computer-based IT in Geography

As mentioned in the previous section, there is a range of software available (see Figure 3.6) and the type of software used will affect the role it has in supporting geographical learning. This role will be considered under two headings: closed, content-bound software and open-ended, content-free (generic) software. The first approach "starts from the *software* and leads into the *curriculum*. Adventure games and simulations come into this category" (Senior, 1990). The second approach "starts from the *curriculum* and then examines the contribution that *software* can make to that curriculum" (Senior, 1990). Both have their uses and each teacher may wish to achieve a balance between the two. However, bearing in mind the comments in Section 2 above, there may be more software of a closed nature at Nursery/Reception working towards more software of an open-ended nature in Year 1/Year 2.

### Closed, Content-bound Software

Examples of this type of software are adventure games and simulations, modelling packages and databases including some CD-ROMs. Some closed programs have geographical content such as "Albert's House", "My World", "Our School", "Little Red Riding Hood" and "Teddy Bear's Picnic". The clearest geographical link is the way in which many of them show places in a mapped form, or encourage children to follow routes and locate hidden objects. Otherwise, it has to be said that the range of such programs for key stage 1 geography is limited. As one of the teachers interviewed said, "What we need are higher quality programs which extend vocabulary, imagination and learning."

### Open-ended, Content-free Software

Examples of this type of software are data handling packages such as "Our Facts", "First Facts", "Grass" and "List Explorer"; wordprocessing packages such as "Folio", "Write-on", "Phases"; Logo programming packages such as "Tiny Logo", "Mazes", "Pip", "Pixie" (table-top "Pip"), "Roamer"; and Photo-CDs.

Photo-CDs are an excellent way of introducing young children to CD-based technology. Basically, a Photo-CD looks like an audio CD or a CD-ROM but, instead of storing sound, it stores images – typically up to 100 on each disc. To use a Photo-CD you need a Photo-CD player, a television screen, and a Photo-CD which contains digitised images of the photographs you would like to use. A blank Photo-CD costs about £4.99 and is available from Boots where your photographs can be transferred on to the Photo-CD at a cost of 60p per image. Any image can be displayed in a second, using a Photo-CD player.

The beauty of this technology is that it is a convenient and safe way to store images. It also provides easy and fast access to your images (each image is numbered). Depending on the quality of the Photo-CD player (details are given in Section 4 below), children will be able to select images to view manually or the teacher can programme the machine to play numbered images in a certain sequence, and so on. As a means of accessing photographs taken by teachers and/or children in and around the locality this has exciting possibilities. Finally, if the Photo-CD player is connected to a computer and you have the correct software it is possible to enlarge and print images or sections of images as needed.

### An Example Using a Database

"The presentation of data through electronic means is a bonus for geography and helps pupils to spend more time on analysing their results than, say, drawing a block graph or pie chart" (Foley & Janikoun, 1992). The purpose of a database is to store, order, group or classify, count and rearrange information. Depending on the program used, the variety of functions will be more or less sophisticated. A simple database is all that is needed at key stage 1. The way a database works is shown in Figure 3.7. The example given relates to a Year 2 mini-topic on Shops and Shopping (see the key stage plan, in Figure 2.6). In a database such as "Our Facts", information can be sorted under pre-defined headings:

*Datafile*: A set of shops in a survey of local streets, together with all the information on the shops.
*Record:* A set of observations made on one shop. Each shop is a "Record" which has information under several headings or "Fields".
*Field:* A particular observation made, or data collected. (In this case there are five fields – *name* (or number), *type, shoppers* (number of), *open hour* (hours the shop opens, to include closed down, if appropriate) and *street*.

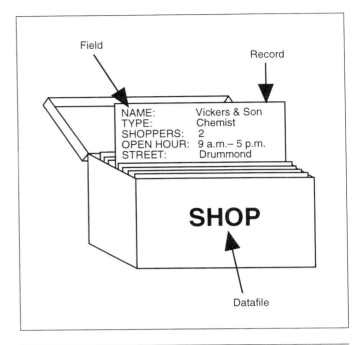

*Figure 3.7 Database for shop survey (adapted from Bowden, 1995,* Primary Geographer, *20).*

Bar charts, pie charts, Venn diagrams and pictograms can be produced once the data is entered. The children can then be encouraged to interpret these charts which should lead to interrogation of the data by asking questions such as:

1. What type of shops open for long hours?
2. What types of shop are found away from the High Street?
3. In which street are most of the shops that are closed found?
4. How many shops that are closed were once food shops?

An example of a shop survey data collection sheet can be found in Supplementary Material 15.

Figure 3.8 gives further examples of computer-based activities that can help meet the five basic objectives outlined in Figure 3.3.

To sum up, there are some things that a computer does very well, "but there are often occasions when children will learn more by other means. The use of software needs to be properly integrated with the whole range of other classroom resources" (Straker, 1989).

| How can computer-based IT help pupils' learning in geography? | Examples of activities which might contribute to a pupil's entitlement to IT in geography. |
|---|---|
| 1. By enhancing their skills of geographical enquiry. | An example of this is the shop survey on page 12 and SM 15. |
| 2. By using a range of information to develop geographical knowledge. | Use a database that has information already stored, perhaps by another class who did a survey of houses in the area.<br>Use the file to get information about houses and to generate further questions for enquiry.<br>Use a pre-programmed database (Branch) to sort farm animals. Add some more animals to the list and create questions to sort them. |
| 3. By developing understanding of geographical patterns and relationships. | Go for a "whisper" walk around the school. Teacher leads and whispers: "We're going *across* the playground, we're turning *left* to the child behind who has to pass it on down the line.<br>In class make a sequence of instructions to move a "Pip" or "Roamer" around the school.<br>The compilation of databases, such as the shop survey (Supplementary Material 15) will encourage children to see patterns and relationships. |
| 4. By experiencing images of people, places and environments. | Use program such as "My World" to plan, e.g. a street. Discuss locations of features in the street: Where should the garage/the pedestrian crossing go? Relate this to locations of features in children's own environment. |
| 5. By increasing awareness of the impact of IT on the changing world. | Collect pictures and information about places where computers are now used in daily life – for leisure or work. Create a display. Make another display to show what used to be used instead. Consider the effects computers have had on our lives. |

*Figure 3.8 Examples of computer-based activities.*

## Section 4: Resources for Information Technology and Geography

The Geographical Association/NCET leaflet, *Primary Geography, a pupil's entitlement to IT* presents information under two useful headings: "Who can help?" and "Where can I find help?".

The following are listed under the first heading:

1. IT co-ordinator.
2. LEA Adviser (IT and Geography).
3. A local IT centre.
4. Expertise in your school cluster.
5. The Geographical Association.
6. National Council for Educational Technology.
7. Micros and Primary Education.
8. Local initial teacher education institution.

Under the second heading "Where can I find help?" the following are listed:

1. Key stages 1 and 2 information technology.
2. The new requirements (SCAA, 1995).
3. Approaches to IT capability.
4. Key stages 1 and 2 (GA/NCET, 1995).
5. *Primary Geographer* (GA magazine).

## Other Types of Resources are Hardware and Software

### Hardware

1. A video recorder.
2. A camcorder.
3. A tape cassette recorder.
4. At least one computer per class.
5. One printer per class (some are in colour).
6. Concept keyboards.
7. Programmable toys.
8. Some toys that respond to commands (e.g. that move when you clap your hands).
9. A Photo-CD player.
10. A CD-ROM player.

### Software

It is difficult to be specific about software because not all packages are available for all makes of hardware. The only suggestion, therefore, is for individual schools to review the current software and look through software catalogues to try to ensure that a range of software packages, such as the following, are available:

1. Adventure games.
2. Simulations.

→

3. Drill/practice programs.
4. Graphics programs.
5. Modelling programs.
6. Logo programs.
7. Wordprocessing programs.
8. Databases.
9. Spreadsheets.
10. Branch programs.

When choosing new programs to support geography teaching and learning, ask yourself the following questions:

1. If it is content-bound, is the geographical content appropriate for key stage 1?
2. Is the way the program works appropriate for key stage 1?
3. If the program is closed, does it help children to learn a geographical skill, specific geographical vocabulary or any other knowledge?
4. If the program is open, will it help children in the process of enquiry? Does it encourage the children to ask questions and think for themselves?

## Useful Addresses

NCET (National Council for Educational Technology) Milburn Hill Road, Science Park, Coventry CV4 7JJ (Tel: 01203 416994).

The Geographical Association, 343 Fulwood Road, Sheffield Sl0 3BP (Tel: 0114 267 0666).

SCAA (Schools Curriculum and Assessment Authority), Newcombe House, 45 Notting Hill Gate, London W11 3JB.

*Publishers:*
Advisory Unit for Microtechnology, Endymion Road, Hatfield, Herts AL10 8AU.

Cambridgeshire Software House, The Town Hall, St. Ives, Huntingdon, Cambs PE17 4AL.

4 mation, Linden Lee, Rock Park, Barnstaple, Devon EX32 9AQ.

Longman Logotron, 124 Cambridge Science Park, Milton Road, Cambridge CB4 4ZS.

Microsoft, Microsoft Place, Winnesh, Wokingham, Berks RG11 5TP.

MUSE (Microcomputer Users in Education) PO Box 43, Houghton on the Hill, Leicestershire LE7 9GX.

Newman College Computer Centre, Genners Lane, Bartley Green, Birmingham B3T 3NT.

Northampton Computer Education Centre Teachers' Centre, Barry Road, Northampton NN1 5JS.

Philip Harris Education, Lynn Lane, Shenton, Lichfield, Staffs WS14 0EE.

Research Machines Ltd, 1 Mill Street, Oxford OX2 0BW.

Sherston Software, Swan Barton, Malmsbury, Wilts SN16 0LH.

Tediman Software, PO Box 23, Southampton SO9 7BD.

For teachers in LEA-supported schools it is always worth contacting your LEA/county adviser or advisory teacher for IT. They will be able to give information about the support that is available from the LEA, the licences held for certain pieces of software, and so on.

## Useful Reading

Crompton, R. (1989) *Computers and the Primary Curriculum 3 – 13,* The Falmer Press.
Koshy, V. and Dodds, P. (1995) *Making IT Work For You: Information Technology Across the Primary Curriculum,* Stanley Thornes.
Senior, S. (1989) *Using IT Across the National Curriculum,* Owlet Books.
Straker, A. (1989) *Children Using Computers,* Blackwell Education.

## Photo-CD Technology

Photo-CDs are available from Boots stores at the photographic counter. Figure 3.9 indicates the range of functions available on Photo-CD machines. The prices are steadily falling as this technology becomes more widely used. So, shop around – bargains are available.

## CD-ROM Suppliers

The Geographical Association supplies lists of CD-ROM suppliers. One is given as Figure 3.10.

---

**Photo-CD player features**

**Autoplay:** Displays the picture in sequence for about 2 seconds each.

**FPS:** (Favourite Picture Selection.) Puts your pictures into your favourite viewing order.

**Frame:** Shows the area of the picture that will be magnified when the Tele button is pressed.

**Full:** Shows the entire picture on a smaller scale with a black border around it.

**Insert:** Allows you to indicate where you want to insert a picture into the FPS memory.

**Interval:** Displays one of 3 times for autoplay – 2, 4 or 8 seconds. The time refers to how long the picture will be on the screen before the next picture appears.

**Rotate:** Rotates a picture clockwise or counter-clockwise.

**Norm:** Shows a picture which fills the screen. A small part of the picture is cropped and not visible.

**Tele:** Enlarges that portion of the picture within the frame.

---

*Figure 3.9 Examples of Photo-CD functions.*

---

**Anglia TV Ltd.**
*General enquiries:*
Anglia TV Ltd.
Anglia House
Norwich NR1 3JE
Tel: 01268 755811
*Software purchase:*
SCA (Anglia Televison)
PO Box 18
Benfleet
Essex SS7 1AZ
Tel: 01286 755811

**Attica**
Unit 21, Kings Meadow
Ferry Hinksey Road
Oxford OX2 ODP
Tel: 01865 791346

**AU Enterprises Ltd.**
(aka Advisory Unit: Computers in Education)
1267 Great North Road
Hatfield
Herts AL9 5JZ
Tel: 01707 266714

**AVP**
School Hill Centre
Chepstow
Gwent NP6 5PH
Tel: 01291 625439

**Chadwyk-Healy Ltd.**
The Quorum
Barnwell Road
Cambridge CB5 8SW
Tel: 01223 215512

**Claymore Services Ltd.**
Station House
Whimple
Exeter EX5 2QH
Tel: 01404 823097

**Creative Curriculum Software**
5 Clover Hill Road
Savile Park
Halifax HX1 2YG
Tel: 01422 340524

**Curriculum Development Initiatives**
Endike Resource Centre
Endike Lane
Hull HU6 7UR
Tel: 01482 883666

**Encyclopaedia Britannica International Ltd.**
Carew House
Station Approach
Wallington
Surrey SM6 ODA
Tel: 0181 669 4355

**GINN**
Prebendal House
Parson's Fee
Aylesbury
Bucks HP20 2QZ
Tel: 01296 88411

**Green PC Company Ltd.**
PO Box 79
Winchester
Hants SO23 7SD
Tel: 01962 886485

**ICL**
Classic Centre
Freepost
ICL Education Systems
Manchester M4 3AR
Tel: 0800 252674

**KimTec**
8 Highland
Wimborne
Dorset BH21 2QN
Tel: 01202 88873

**Koch Media**
East Street
Farnham
Surrey GU9 7XX
Tel: 01252 714340

**Nelson Multimedia**
PO Box 1487
Cheriton House
North Way
Andover
Hants SP10 1YN
Tel: 01264 342992

**Ordnance Survey**
Contact for local stockist:
Education Team
Romsey Road
Southampton SO16 4GU
Tel: 01703 792012

**Pebbleshore**
Lewes Enterprise Centre
112 Malling Street
Lewes
East Sussex BN7 2RJ
Tel: 01273 483890

**Photoair Software Ltd.**
Photoair House
191a Main Street
Yaxley
Peterborough PE7 3LD
Tel: 01733 241850

**TAG Developments Ltd.**
19 High Street
Gravesend
Kent DA11 OBA
Tel: 01474 357350 (Enquiries)
Tel: 0800 591262 (Orderline)

**ULTRALAB**
Anglia Polytechnic University
Sawyers Hall Lane
Brentwood
Essex CM15 9BT
Tel: 01277 200587

**Yorkshire International Thomson Multimedia (YITM)**
Television Centre
104 Kirkstall Road
Leeds LS3 1JS
Tel: 0113 246 1528

---

*Figure 3.10 CD-ROM suppliers (The Geographical Association/NCET, 1995).*

# Matrix for key stage 1 curriculum planning

|  | Reception | Year 1 | Year 2 | Ongoing |
|---|---|---|---|---|
| Autumn |  |  |  |  |
| Spring |  |  |  |  |
| Summer |  |  |  |  |

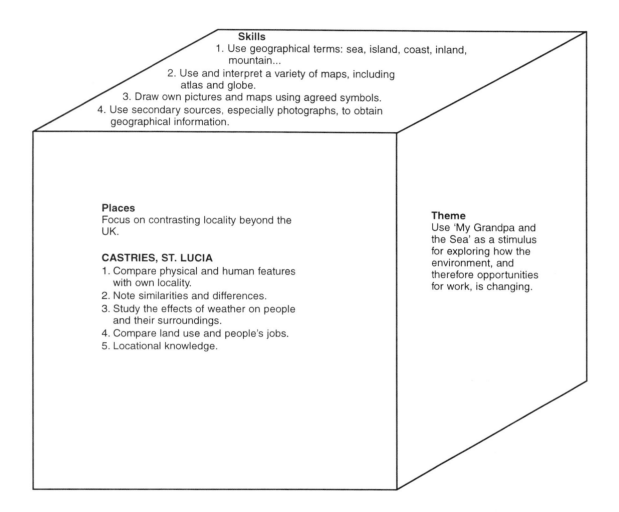

**Skills**
1. Use geographical terms: sea, island, coast, inland, mountain...
2. Use and interpret a variety of maps, including atlas and globe.
3. Draw own pictures and maps using agreed symbols.
4. Use secondary sources, especially photographs, to obtain geographical information.

**Places**
Focus on contrasting locality beyond the UK.

**CASTRIES, ST. LUCIA**
1. Compare physical and human features with own locality.
2. Note similarities and differences.
3. Study the effects of weather on people and their surroundings.
4. Compare land use and people's jobs.
5. Locational knowledge.

**Theme**
Use 'My Grandpa and the Sea' as a stimulus for exploring how the environment, and therefore opportunities for work, is changing.

Use the information above to plan a scheme of work for geography over a period of six weeks.

| | | Key questions | Learning outcomes: knowledge, skills, understanding & attitudes | Pupil activities: (teaching & teaching strategies) & use of IT | Resources | Assessment opportunities | PoS |
|---|---|---|---|---|---|---|---|
| Topic _____ | Age group _____ | | | | | | |
| Subject _____ | Key stage _____ | | | | | | |
| | Focus _____ | | | | | | |

*Martin: Teaching Early Years Geography*

*Chris Kington Publishing*

| Objectives and National Curriculum PoS | Enquiry route | Activities | Organisation and assessment opportunities |
|---|---|---|---|
| | 1. Ask questions | | |
| | 2. Plan | | |
| | 3. Investigate | | |
| | 4. Evaluate | | |

1. What lies in the area (within walking distance)?
2. What can be viewed from the area? (Is there a natural viewpoint? What does the skyline show?)
3. What is special and recognisable about this place? (The distinctive human and physical featues that give the place its character.)

Bearing in mind the questions above, walk your area. Make an inventory of what is there and what is accessible to children (make use of maps and aerial photographs if you have them).

Using the National Curriculum for geography, examine the match between the PoS, LDs and your inventory.

**Make a list of geographical vocabulary relevant to your area under the headings: physical, human, environmental.**

On an A4 sheet, define your local area using the suggested format below (from NCC INSET materials, 1993).

---

**Local area**

How would you define your local area?

_____

_____

_____

_____

_____

Draw a sketch of the area to show the main features of your locality.

Key:

Additional information

_____

_____

_____

_____

_____

---

| Progression in skills | |
|---|---|
| **Level 1** | Pupils *use* resources provided and their own *observations* to respond to questions about places. |
| **Level 2** | Pupils *select* information from resources provided. They *use* this information and their own *observations* to *ask* and *respond* to questions about places. They begin to use *appropriate vocabulary*. |
| **Level 3** | Pupils *use skills* and sources of evidence to *respond* to a range of *geographical questions*. |
| **Level 4** | Pupils *suggest suitable geographical questions* for study. They *use a range of geographical skills* and evidence to investigate places and themes. They *communicate* their findings using *appropriate geographical vocabulary*. |


| **Topic** | **Focus** |
|---|---|
| **Skills** | **Level 1** |
| | **Level 2** |
| | **Level 3** |

| Progression in environmental awareness | |
|---|---|
| **Level 1** | Pupils *express their views* on features of the environment of a locality that they find *attractive or unattractive.* |
| **Level 2** | Pupils *express views* on *attractive or unattractive* features of the environment of a locality. (In this case, the views need not be their own, working towards objectivity.) |
| **Level 3** | Pupils *offer reasons* for some of their *judgements* about places. |
| **Level 4** | Pupils *describe* how people can both *improve* and *damage* the environment. |

| Topic | Focus |
|---|---|
| **Environmental awareness** | **Level 1** |
| | **Level 2** |
| | **Level 3** |

Formative teachers assessment record     R ☐     Y1 ☐     Y2 ☐

Name: _____      Date: _____

Activity: _____

| Possible outcomes |
|---|
|  |

| Account | Interpretation | Action |
|---|---|---|
|  |  |  |

Comments:

| Geographical activity | IT activity |
|---|---|
| Skills of geographical enquiry. | |
| Use a range of information sources to develop geographical knowledge. | |
| Develop understanding of geographical patterns and relationships. | |
| Experience images of people, places and environments. | |
| Increase awareness of the impact of IT on the changing world. | |

*Martin: Teaching Early Years Geography*

*Chris Kington Publi*

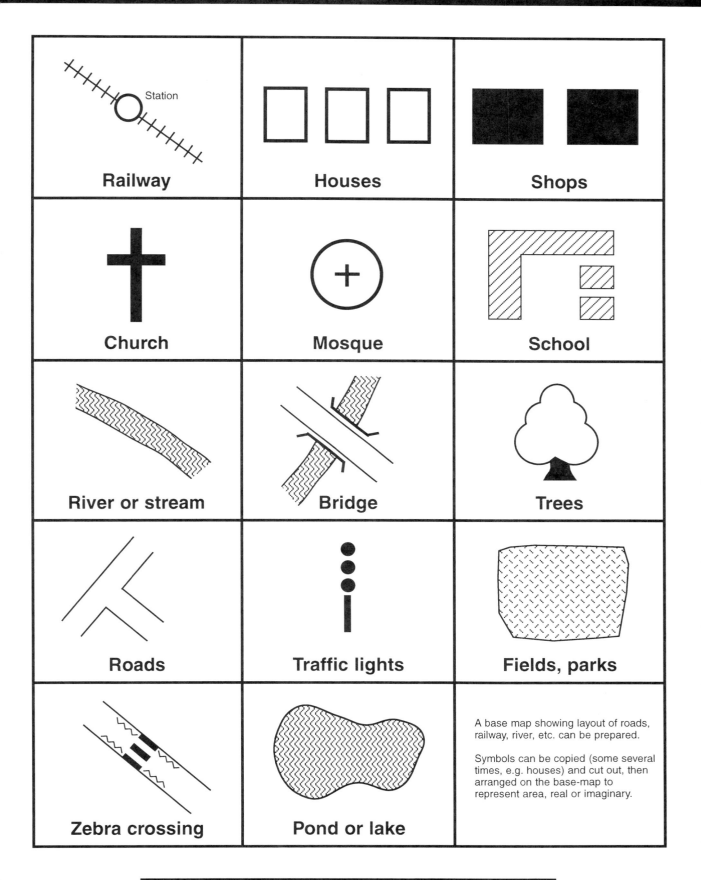

| Railway | Houses | Shops |
| --- | --- | --- |
| Church | Mosque | School |
| River or stream | Bridge | Trees |
| Roads | Traffic lights | Fields, parks |
| Zebra crossing | Pond or lake | A base map showing layout of roads, railway, river, etc. can be prepared.<br><br>Symbols can be copied (some several times, e.g. houses) and cut out, then arranged on the base-map to represent area, real or imaginary. |

Use this map to:

1. Photocopy for children to label the constituent countries, where they live, etc.

2. Enlarge to A3. Stick on card. Colour constituent countries in contrasting colours. Laminate. Cut out countries. Give to children as jig-saw on base outline, A3, also laminated.

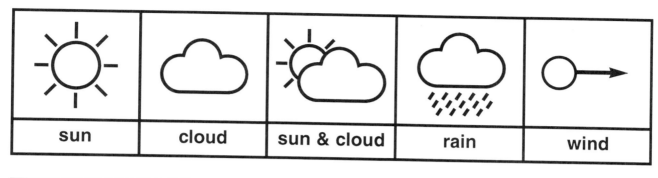

| sun | cloud | sun & cloud | rain | wind |

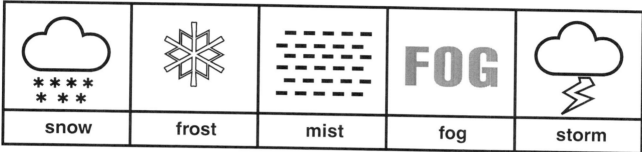

| snow | frost | mist | fog | storm |

Use these symbols to record the weather over a period of 3–4 weeks

| | | | | |
|---|---|---|---|---|
| | | | | |
| **Monday** | **Tuesday** | **Wednesday** | **Thursday** | **Friday** |

At the end of the time, cut up the symbols and rearrange on a chart like this:

Display for all the class to read and interpret. What sort of weather have we had most/least? Why?

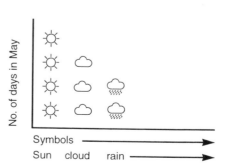

Source: SEAC KS1 SAT materials (1993).

*rtin: Teaching Early Years Geography*

*Chris Kington Publishing*

1. Each group receives a character card:

   Grandfather, 75 years old
   Grandmother, 63 years old
   Aunty, 27 years old
   Dad, 30 years old
   Teenager, 16 years old
   Child, 9 years old
   Toddler, 3 years old

2. For your character decide:

   a) What sort of person he or she is.
   b) Whether they have children or grandchildren.
   c) A list of things they do when they go to the park, e.g. the grandmother might chat with friends, take grandchildren to feed the ducks, sit and read, etc.

3. Once you have made your list of things your character does in the park, write another list of the things she or he would need in order to be able to do these things. For example, the grandmother might need benches to sit on, the children need swings to play on, a pond is needed for the ducks, etc.

4. Using your second list, and the outline plan of the park, make a plan of your character's ideal park. Think carefully where you put things and why you put them there. You may want to do a draft plan first, and then do a neat copy on a large sheet of paper. Use the class agreed symbols where necessary.

5. Compare your plan with another group's.

   a) Are they both the same?
   b) Why not?
   c) What is the same/different?
   d) Why are they different?

If you were a planner and had been asked to plan a park suitable for all the people in the town, what would you do before making your plan?

Children could also be given the opportunity to question each other about why they put certain things in the location they did and whether or not they considered safety.

*Martin: Teaching Early Years Geography*

*Chris Kington Publish*

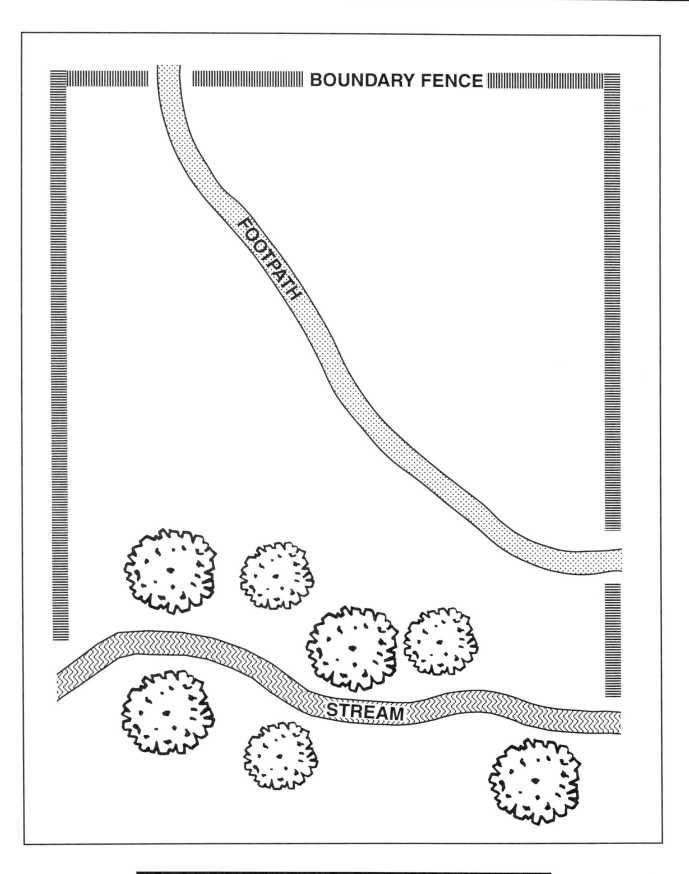

*rtin: Teaching Early Years Geography*          *Chris Kington Publishing*

**Shop survey**

**Locality of** _____ **school**

**Name of street** _____

| Shop No. | | | | | | | | |
|---|---|---|---|---|---|---|---|---|
| **Shop type** | | | | | | | | |
| Baker | | | | | | | | |
| Butcher | | | | | | | | |
| Grocer | | | | | | | | |
| Greengrocer | | | | | | | | |
| Newsagent | | | | | | | | |
| Post Office | | | | | | | | |
| Chemist | | | | | | | | |
| Hairdresser | | | | | | | | |
| Take-away | | | | | | | | |
| Clothes | | | | | | | | |
| Other | | | | | | | | |
| **Number of shoppers** | | | | | | | | |
| **Opening times** | | | | | | | | |
| 9 a.m.–5 p.m. | | | | | | | | |
| 9 a.m.–5.30 p.m. | | | | | | | | |
| 7 a.m.–2 p.m. | | | | | | | | |
| 7 a.m.–7p.m. | | | | | | | | |
| Other | | | | | | | | |
| Closed down | | | | | | | | |

(A quick survey beforehand by the teacher will indicate the opening times required.)

| Shop number | Shop name |
|---|---|
| 1. | |
| 2. | |
| 3. | |
| 4. | |
| 5. | |
| 6. | |

**THIS PAGE MAY BE PHOTOCOPIED FOR USE IN SCHOOL**

*Martin: Teaching Early Years Geography*                    *Chris Kington Publis*

| Room | Number | Telephone ☎ |
|---|---|---|
| Sitting room | | |
| Dining room | | |
| Kitchen | | |
| Bedroom | | |
| Bathroom | | |
| Toilet | | |
| Playroom | | |
| Study | | |
| Other | | |
| | | |

## References and Bibliography

Bale, J. (1987) *Geography in the Primary School*, London, Routledge & Kegan Paul.

Ball, C. (1994) *Start Right: The Importance of Early Learning*, London, RSA.

Bennett, N., Desforges, C., Cockburn, A. and Wilkinson, B. (1984) *The Quality of Pupil Learning Experiences*, London LEA.

Bennetts, T. (1995) 'Continuity and progression', *Primary Geography*, 21, pp. 44–45.

Bowden, D. (1991) 'IT: Off the shelf or self help', *Primary Geographer*, 6, p. 11.

Bowden, D. (1995) 'Bringing IT down to earth', *Primary Geographer*, 20, p. 25.

Bruner, J. (1966) *Towards a Theory of Instruction*, Cambridge, Mass, Harvard University Press.

Catling, S. (1978) 'The child's spatial conception and geographical experience', *Journal of Geography*, 77, 1, pp. 24–28.

Catling, S. (1992) *Placing Places*, Sheffield, The Geographical Association.

Catling, S. (1992) *Mapstart 1, 2 & 3*, London, Collins Longman.

Catling, S. (1995) 'Wider Horizons: the children's charter', *Primary Geography*, 20, pp. 4–6.

CCW (1991) *Geography National Curriculum for Wales, Non-Statutory Guidance*, Cardiff, Welsh Office.

David, T., Curtis, A. and Siraj-Blatchford, I. (1992) *Effective Teaching in the Early Years: Fostering Children's Learning in Nurseries and Infant Classes*, an OMEP (UK) report, Stoke-on-Trent, Trentham Books.

DES (1985) *Curriculum Matters: The Curriculum 5–13*, London, HMSO.

DES (1989) *Curriculum Matters 15: Information Technology 5–13*, London, HMSO.

DES (1990a) *Geography for Ages 5–16: Proposals of the Secretary of State for Education and Science and the Secretary of State for Wales*, London, HMSO.

DES (1990b) *Starting With Quality: The Rumbold Report*, London, HMSO.

DES (1991) *Geography in the National Curriculum*, London, HMSO.

DFE (1995a) *Geography in the National Curriculum*, London, HMSO.

DFE (1995b) *Information Technology in the National Curriculum*, London, HMSO.

Egan, K. (1988) *Teaching as Storytelling*, London, Routledge.

Fien, J. and Gerber, R. (1988) *Teaching Geography for a Better World*, London, Oliver & Boyd.

Foley, M. and Janikoun, J. (1992) *The Really Practical Guide to Teaching Geography*, Cheltenham, Stanley Thornes.

GA/NCET (1995) *Primary Geography: A Pupil's Entitlement to IT*, Sheffield, The Geographical Association/National Council for Educational Technology.

Knight, P. (1993) *Primary Geography, Primary History*, London, David Fulton.

Koshy, V. and Dodds, P. (1995) *Making IT Work for You*, Cheltenham, Stanley Thornes.

Mackintosh, M. (1995) 'Revising Courses at Key Stage 1', *Primary Geographer* 21, pp. 12–14.

Makins, V. (1995) 'Licence to convert to a waiting room', *Times Educational Supplement*, June 23.

Matthews, M. (1992) *Making Sense of Place*, Lewes, Harvester – Wheatsheaf, Barnes & Noble.

May, S. and Cook, J. (1993) *Fieldwork in Action 2: An Enquiry Approach*, Sheffield, The Geographical Association.

May, S., Richardson, P. and Banks, V. (1993) *Fieldwork in Action 1: Planning Fieldwork*, Sheffield, Geographical Association.

Milner, A. (1994) *Geography Starts Here! Practical Approaches with Nursery and Reception Children*, Sheffield, The Geographical Association.

Mitchell, C. and Koshy, V. (1993) *Effective Teacher Assessment: Looking at Children's Learning in the Primary Classroom*, London, Hodder & Stoughton.

Morgan, W. (1991) A Guide to The Geographical Association's '*Geographical Work in Primary and Middle Schools* (Mills 1988)' for Teachers Implementing National Curriculum Geography at Key Stages 1 and 2, Sheffield, The Geographical Association.

Morgan, W. (1992) *Focus on Castries St. Lucia*, Sheffield, The Geographical Association.

Morgan, W. (1995) 'The shape of things to come – a summary of the changes', *Primary Geographer* 21, pp. 10-11.

NCC (1993) *Teaching Geography at Key Stages 1 and 2: An INSET Guide*, York, NCC.

Norris-Nicholson, H. (1994) *Place in Story-Time*, Sheffield, The Geographical Association.

OFSTED (1995) *Geography: A Review of Inspection Findings 1993/94*, London, HMSO.

Palmer, J. (1994) *Geography in the Early Years*, London, Routledge.

Plowden, (1967) *Children and Their Primary Schools: A Report for the Central Advisory Council for Education*, London, HMSO.

Russell, K. (1995) 'IT and geography in the revised curriculum', *Primary Geographer*, 21, pp. 39–41.

SCAA (1995) *Planning the Curriculum at Key Stages 1 and 2*, London, SCAA.

Scoffham, S. and Jewson, T. (1994) "First steps in using photographs", *Primary Geographer*, 7, p. 2.

Scoffham (1995) 'Local Investigations', *Primary Geographer* 21, pp. 42–43.

Scott, J. (1994) 'Geography in the Nursery: Where's Spot?', *Primary Geographer*, 18, p. 21.

SEAC (1993) *Children's Work Assessed at Key Stage 1: Geography and History*, London, SEAC.

Sebba, J. (1995) *Geography for All*, London, David Fulton.

Senior, S. (1990) *Using IT Across the National Curriculum*, Owlet Books.

Siegal, A. W. and Schadler, M. (1977) 'Young children's cognitive maps of their classroom', *Child Development*, 48, pp. 388–94.

Smith, S. and Richardson, P. (1995) 'Access for all: special educational needs', *Primary Geographer*, 21, pp. 36–38.

Straker, A. (1989) *Children Using Computers*, Oxford, Blackwell.

TGAT (1988) *National Curriculum Task Group on Assessment and Testing: A Report*, London, HMSO.

Wiegand, P. (1992) *Places in the Primary School*, Lewes, Falmer Press.

Wiegand, P. (1993) *Children and Primary Geography*, London, Cassell.

# Index